Praise for *Elite Capture*

"I was waiting for this book without this book." —**Ruth Wilson Gilmor**
Racial Capitalism and the *Case for A*

"Olúfẹ́mi O. Táíwò is a thinker on fire. He not only calls out empire for shrouding its bloodied hands in the cloth of magical thinking but calls on all of us to do the same. Elite capture, after all, is about turning oppression and its cure into a (neo)liberal commodity exchange where identities become capitalism's latest currency rather than the grounds for revolutionary transformation. The lesson is clear: only when we think for ourselves and act with each other, together in deep, dynamic, and difficult solidarity, can we begin to remake the world." —**Robin D. G. Kelley**, author of *Freedom Dreams: The Black Radical Imagination*

"Olúfẹ́mi O. Táíwò's book is worth sitting with and absorbing. While critically examining what happens when elites hijack our critiques and terminologies for their own interests, *Elite Capture* acutely reminds us that building power globally means we think and build outside of our internal confines. That is when we have the greatest possibility at worldmaking." —**Ibram X. Kendi**, National Book Award–winning author of *Stamped from the Beginning* and *How to Be an Antiracist*

"Olúfẹ́mi O. Táíwò offers an indispensable and urgent set of analyses, interventions, and alternatives to "identity politics," "centering," and much more. The book offers a sober assessment of the state of our racial politics and a powerful path on how to build the world that we deserve." —**Derecka Purnell**, author of *Becoming Abolitionists*

"With global breadth, clarity, and precision, Olúfẹ́mi O. Táíwò dissects the causes and consequences of elite capture and charts an alternative constructive politics for our time. The result is an erudite yet accessible book that draws widely on the rich traditions of black and anti-colonial political thought." —**Adom Getachew**, author of *Worldmaking after Empire: The Rise and Fall of Self-Determination*

"Among the churn of books on 'wokeness' and 'political correctness,' philosopher Olúfẹ́mi O. Táíwò's *Elite Capture* clearly stands out. With calm, clarity, erudition, and authority, Táíwò walks the reader through the morass, deftly explicating the distinction between substantive and worthy critique and weaponized backlash. Understanding the culture wars is essential to US politics right now, and no one has done it better than Táíwò in this book." —**Jason Stanley**, author of *How Fascism Works*

"Olúfẹ́mi O. Táíwò is one of the great social theorists of our generation. *Elite Capture* is a brilliant, devastating book. Táíwò deploys his characteristic blend of philosophical rigor, sociological insight, and political clarity to reset the debate on identity politics. Táíwò shows how the structure of racial capitalism, not misguided activism, is today's prime threat to egalitarian, antiracist politics. And Táíwò's suggested path forward, a constructive and materialist politics at the radical edge of the possible, is exactly what we need to escape these desperate times. Anyone concerned with dismantling inequalities and building a better world needs to read this book." —**Daniel Aldana Cohen**, coauthor of *A Planet to Win: Why We Need a Green New Deal*

"Táíwò's book is an insightful and fascinating look at how it is that elites capture and subvert efforts to better society. Anyone who wants to understand and improve upon the activist movements shaking our world needs to read this book." —**Liam Kofi Bright**, assistant professor at the London School of Economics

"This book, building on one of the most lucid, powerful, and important essays I can recall reading in recent years, is, in a word, brilliant. Read it—and read it twice. Every sentence contains multitudes." —**Daniel Denvir**, host of *The Dig*

Elite
Capture

How the Powerful
Took Over Identity Politics
(and Everything Else)

Olúfẹ́mi O. Táíwò

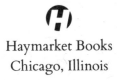

Haymarket Books
Chicago, Illinois

Published in 2022 by
Haymarket Books
P.O. Box 180165
Chicago, IL 60618
773-583-7884
www.haymarketbooks.org
info@haymarketbooks.org

ISBN: 978-1-642596-88-5

Distributed to the trade in the US through Consortium Book Sales
and Distribution (www.cbsd.com) and internationally through
Ingram Publisher Services International
(www.ingramcontent.com).

This book was published with the generous support of Lannan
Foundation and Wallace Action Fund.

Special discounts are available for bulk purchases by organizations
and institutions. Please email info@haymarketbooks.org for more
information.

Cover design by Steve Leard.

Printed in Canada by union labor.

Library of Congress Cataloging-in-Publication data is available.

10 9 8 7 6 5 4 3

Contents

Acknowledgments

As always, I have an uncountable number of people to thank for this work.

Thanks to my family for their support: my siblings Ibukun and Ebun, and my parents Abiola and Yetunde, all the Taiwos and Sokunbis, and all the Cincinnati Nigerians; Abigail Higgins, the Higginses, and the Kennedys.

I'd like to thank my editor, Emma Young, and Haymarket's, Sam Smith, as well as all those who helped make the logistics of this book possible: Anthony Arnove, Stephanie Steiker, Suzanne Lipinska and those at KIOSK and Africasia who made her journalistic work available to me, including Simon Delobel and Mathieu Kleyebe Abonnenc. This book grew out of two essays published at *Boston Review* and *The Philosopher*. I want to thank Deb Chasman, Matt Lord, and their colleagues at *Boston*, as well as Chiara Ricciardone and Anthony Morgan and their colleagues at *The Philosopher* for their support on the initial versions of this idea, which made this book possible.

A special thanks to supportive scholars whose direct and indirect support made it possible for me to be here at all: AJ Julius, Daniela Dover, Melvin Rogers, Jason Stanley, Gaye Theresa Johnson, and folks whose work, teaching, or leadership I leaned on implicitly or explicitly: Josh Armstrong, Quill Kukla, Mark Lance, Bryce Huebner, Henry Richardson. To friends and comrades whose support and advice was were just as essential to making it through the writing: Liam Kofi Bright, Marques Vestal, Thabisile Griffin, Austin Branion, Alexis Cooke, Shelbi Nahwilet Meissner, Joel Michael "Boxcutter Joelie" Reynolds, Jeanne-Marie Jackson-Awotwi.

To the institutions and organizations I have able to learn in and from: The Undercommons, UAW 2865, UCLA Labor Center, LA Black Workers Center, and Pan-African Community Action.

To our moral ancestors, without whose struggle and sacrifice none of this would be possible: to the anti-colonial fighters, to the abolitionists, to the workers who demanded more, and to the activists who refused to accept less.

To all of our moral and genealogical descendants, to those who are yet young and those who are yet to come: with love, with hope, and with solidarity.

Introduction

"There is no racism, no tribalism; we are not struggling merely so that we may have a flag, an anthem and ministers. We are not going to install ourselves in the Governors' palace, that is not our objective.... We are struggling to liberate our people not only from colonialism but also from any form of exploitation.

We want no one to exploit our people any more, neither whites nor blacks."

—Amílcar Cabral, *Unity and Struggle*[1]

The beginning of the pandemic lockdowns in the spring of 2020 announced lulls in much of business as usual: public transportation, interstate travel, nightlife, community programming, libraries, barbershops. Even playgrounds went silent. But it did not stop police murders around the globe.

In some cases, the lockdowns even set the killings into motion: on March 31, four days after Kenya's curfew began, Kenyan police officers enforced the order by storming a neighborhood and beating people indiscriminately, eventually opening fire with live ammunition.[2] One of these bullets struck and killed Yasin Hussein Moyo, a thirteen-year-old looking down onto the fracas from his apartment balcony. On May 19, twenty-one-year-old Anderson Arboleda was chased by two police officers in Puerto Tejada, Colombia, for breaking pandemic curfew. He was beaten and pepper-sprayed so severely that he died the next morning.[3]

In other cases, the pandemic simply failed to sufficiently disrupt the normal patterns of police violence: on May 18, three police officers entered a home in Rio de Janeiro's Complexo do Salgueiro favela where six cousins were playing together.[4] They opened fire, shooting fourteen-year-old João Pedro Matos Pinto in the back. A relative drove him to a police helicopter in a desperate attempt to get him medical care. The family knew neither his whereabouts nor his medical condition until seventeen hours later—when they found his body at the coroner. By Rio de Janeiro police's own estimates, they killed an average of six people per day in early 2020; if these killings followed the pattern of the past decade, more than three quarters of the dead were Black men.[5] For a sense of scale: there were nearly twice as many police killings in the single Brazilian state of Rio de Janeiro in 2019 as there were across the entire United States in that same year.[6]

In the United States, a spate of police killings whose victims included Breonna Taylor (March 13), George Floyd (May 25), and Tony McDade (May 27) launched a volume of protest unprecedented in US history: by some estimates, as many as twenty-six million people in the country participated in one form or another, a figure that would represent nearly 8 percent of the entire US population.[7] The protests were not only large, but combative. Across the country, luxury malls and retail stores were sacked and pillaged. In Minneapolis, police fled the Third Precinct for their lives as rebels smashed windshields with projectiles and set the building on fire.

The protests were global in scope. In June 2020, demonstrators took to the streets in cities across the world, including Rio, Seoul, London, Sydney, and Monrovia.[8] This global solidarity undoubtedly owes itself to the steadfast international organizing work of Black Lives Matter chapters, the umbrella Movement for Black Lives, and a number of other organizations around the world working in partnership and solidarity with them. But it also is rooted in the global nature of the intersecting dynamics of racism and policing. These problems are among the many legacies of our immediate past that shape our lives today.

In Nigeria, the energy crested a few months later, in October 2020, when protestors took to the streets to call for the abolition of the country's Special Anti-robbery Squad (SARS), a secretive police force that has been responsible for waves of extrajudicial torture, sexual assault, and murder of Nigerians. The #EndSARS protestors were met with bitter resistance—and live ammunition—from the Nigerian government, including during the infamous Lekki Toll Gate massacre. Amnesty International put the death toll at twelve.[9] It is important to understand that the #EndSARS protesters were not merely sympathetic to, or influenced by, other protests earlier in the year, but were fighting on their own front in the same struggle.

Nigeria's Special Anti-robbery Squad, US police forces, and many other repressive bodies use similar ideological structures and strategies of violence because they are similar kinds of institutions, created to achieve similar aims. Most of these forces have their roots in the colonial era of the nineteenth and twentieth centuries, when national-level institutions functioned like franchises under the global racial empire's logo, each territorial army, colonial government, and national stock exchange linked together in a powerful cartel. While individual security forces were dedicated to different national interests under the global racial empire, the cartel as a whole served the interests of the same elites, making sure wealth and advantage flowed south to north, Black to white. That system has never been dismantled. So, while "empire" is no longer a popular term in global politics, we're still basically living it: nakedly imperial structures live on in forms like France's management of currencies of many of its former African colonies, and seemingly neutral international corporations and institutions bully the poorer peoples and countries of the world in "neocolonial" fashion.[10]

So, despite differences in local context, when people around the world rose up against the police terror and violence to which they have been subjected for hundreds of years, it was immediately clear that something global was at stake. The response from governing elites was equally immediate: the World Bank established a "Task Force on Racism," and the United Nations, under pressure from the entire African Union bloc of fifty-four countries, agreed to launch a yearlong inquiry into anti–Black racism.[11]

Two strategic trends in the response quickly became clear: the elites' tactic of performing symbolic identity politics to pacify protestors without enacting material reforms; and their efforts to rebrand (not replace) existing institutions, also using elements of identity politics.

In a stunningly clear summary of the first trend, the mayor of Washington, DC, had "Black Lives Matter" painted on streets near the White House, atop which protestors continued to be brutalized. The following year, the Central Intelligence Agency rolled out the second strategy, producing a dozen "Humans of CIA" recruitment videos reaching out to multiple identity groups, including queer and Indigenous people. Journalist Roberto Lovato cautioned readers about the resonance of this moment in an aptly titled article, "The Age of Intersectional Empire Is Upon Us": "In the vast world that lives outside of progressive circles, there are millions of people who have emotional reactions to Army and Marine recruitment ads featuring proud Black and Latinx soldiers."[12]

Formal political task forces, encouraging murals, and inspirational commercials are serviceable carrots. But there's also, of course, the stick. By June 2021, twenty-five state legislatures had introduced legislation to ban the teaching of "critical race theory," as part of a culture war backed by think tanks such as the Heritage Foundation and Manhattan Institute, alongside well-connected individuals such as Mark Meadows (a former White House chief of staff in the Trump administration).[13] In the United Kingdom, the British government formed a Commission on Race and Ethnic Disparities, which released a report exonerating the government of the institutional racism alleged by Black Lives Matter protestors.[14] Where co-optation fails, regular old repression will do.

So what, then, are we to make of identity politics? Some expressions of identity politics are twisted to rebrand old imperial projects, while others are actively banned by the powers that be. Is it itself an innocuously different version of left politics, separated from more orthodox left politics mainly by "failures of communication" as philosopher Ashley Bohrer suggests?[15] Or, more ominously, is identity politics "an essential tool utilized by the bourgeoisie to maintain its class domination over the working class by keeping workers divided along racial and gender lines," as Dominic Gustavo alleges at the *World Socialist Web Site*?[16] Or is identity politics, as embodied in critical race theory, a dangerous ideology and threat to the established order that the powers that be aim to stamp out?

The Combahee River Collective (and Why Identity Politics Isn't What You Think It Is)

The term "identity politics" was first popularized by the 1977 manifesto of the Combahee River Collective, an organization of queer, Black feminist socialists, and it was supposed to be about fostering solidarity and collaboration.

American studies scholar Duchess Harris recounts the collective's origin story as follows: in 1961, President John F. Kennedy convened a Commission on the Status of Women. It was split into four consultative bodies, one of which was the Consultation on Negro Women. This event inspired sequels, and the third National Conference of Commissions on the Status of Women birthed the meeting that founded the National Organization for Women, which founders hoped would serve as an "NAACP for women." However, NOW failed to live up to this promise to treat race seriously—and Black nationalist organizations failed equally to address gender.[17] As a result, in 1973, activists formed the National Black Feminist Organization.[18]

In 1974, the young activist Barbara Smith met Demita Frazier after she began organizing an NBFO chapter in Boston. The pair agreed with many NBFO goals but also wanted an organization that would discuss "radical economics" more freely and that would guarantee a voice for lesbians. And so, from a meeting of four, began the Combahee River Collective. From 1977 to 1980, they held seven retreats with fellow activists, which were attended by like-minded Boston veteran activists, and even the famed writer Audre Lorde.

The experiences that united these activists—the consistent sidelining and devaluation of their political priorities within different political organizations—were foundational to the stance they developed, which they christened "identity politics."

"We, as black women, we actually had a right to create political priorities and agendas and actions and solutions based in our experiences," Smith later explained—a political agenda based in their full experiences and interests, rather than positioning them as white women's tokens or as Black men's secretaries, and one that incorporated the full complexity of their values, rather than a degraded and misshapen caricature of them. As Princeton professor Keeanga-Yamahtta Taylor puts it, "One could not expect Black women to be wholly active in political movements that neither represented nor advanced their interests"; therefore, the identity politics they developed served as "*entry points* for Black women to engage in politics," rather than a whole cloth withdrawal from problematic organizations and movements.[19]

As such, they were in favor of diverse coalitional organizing, an approach that Smith later saw exemplified by the Bernie Sanders presidential campaign's grassroots approach and its focus on social issues that people of many identities face, especially "basic needs of food, housing and healthcare."[20] Beverly Smith, another of the group's founders, recalls the immediate political effect of the group's statement among groups in the Boston left: "[W]e also drew many women of color or who were not Black to us. We had connections with Latinas. We had connections with Asian women. . . . And they drew us too. Because it wasn't just like one way. When we'd find out about things that were happening, we would get ourselves there as well."[21] The collective's principled stance on identity politics functioned as a principle of unity, rather than division.

But, in the decades since the founding of the Combahee River Collective, instead of forging alliances across difference, some have chosen to close ranks—especially on social media—around ever-narrower conceptions of group interests. Smith says, diplomatically, that many of today's common uses of the concept are "very different than what we intended."[22] Asad Haider puts it more starkly in his book *Mistaken Identity,* where he acknowledges the radical history of the concept while nevertheless describing identity politics as "the ideology that emerged to appropriate this emancipatory legacy in service of the advancement of political and economic elites."[23] While agreeing with these points, I also agree with political theorist Marie Moran and philosopher Linda Martín Alcoff who have both argued effectively that ideological explanations that tie troubling political developments to the ideas supposedly built into identity politics tend to miss the mark: many criticisms target ideas that aren't essential to identity-based movements or that misconstrue their basic goals entirely.[24]

The idea of "elite capture" helps reconcile these two points with each other. It is true that recent developments in the meaning and use of identity politics have not stopped police murders or emptied prisons. Identity politics has, however, equipped people, organizations, and institutions with a new vocabulary to describe their politics and aesthetic—even if the substance of those political decisions are irrelevant or even counter to the interests of the marginalized people whose identities are being deployed. But that is a feature of how identity politics is being used, rather than what identity politics is at its core. It is this "elite capture"—not identity politics itself—that stands between us and a transformative, nonsectarian, coalitional politics.

Elite Capture: The Bigger Problem

The concept of elite capture originated in the study of developing countries to describe the way socially advantaged people tend to gain control over financial benefits, especially foreign aid, meant for others. But the concept has also been applied more generally to describe how political projects can be hijacked in principle or in effect by the well positioned and resourced. And yet, the idea also helps to explain how public resources such as knowledge, attention, and values become distorted and distributed by power structures.

Elite capture accounts for many of the common objections leveled against identity politics, including that it requires uncritical support for political figures based on their identities without regard for their politics and that it often reflects social preoccupations that are "really for rich white people." One commentator, Saagar Enjeti, criticized "the identity politics obsessed elite wing of the Democratic party," alleging that "the people who populate our newsrooms" and "populate the professional managerial class . . . have far too much of an impact on our contemporary political discourse."[25] Despite having identified the problem with mainstream popular uses of identity politics today—the outsize impact of well-positioned people on our political discourse—Enjeti nevertheless seems to think this is a special problem of one wing of one political party. In fact, the underlying dynamics are as old as politics itself and are not confined to a particular politics of social identity.

Elite capture is not a conspiracy. It's bigger than cynical appropriations, opportunism, or the moral successes or failures of any individual or group. It is a kind of system behavior—a phenomenon articulated at the population level, an observable (predictable) pattern of actions involving individuals, groups, and subgroups, each of whom may be pursuing any number of different goals from their own narrow point of view. Elite capture is not limited to the scope of their intentions. The constant dynamic of individual and group interactions makes up a social system, and elite capture emerges out of that dynamic.

Systems and systems-level issues are big and complex, but they are not abstract. Social systems are real: after all, we live in them. As such, they are entities that we can observe and, frequently, anticipate. Our social sciences are, for better or worse, attempts to do exactly that. It is of course true that social systems are exceedingly complex—perhaps more so than physical systems, since they encompass them, plus quite a bit more besides. And, since our collective thinking about the system is itself an important part of the system we are analyzing, the very thing that we study shifts as we understand it differently, precisely *because* we understand it differently.

So if elite capture is bigger than the most nefarious plans of the biggest villains, is it also bigger than the best intentions of those who oppose them?

In reality, we may not be able to entirely eliminate elite capture from the world. Achieving radical equality in the distribution of resources and power is itself an idealized outcome of the social movements we support, rather than the sort of thing that could precede and produce their success. Much like rust emerges in different times and places where metal and water meet, elite capture emerges in different times and places where social systems encounter certain conditions (as I explain in chapter 3). But this book is motivated by the belief that when we can recognize elite capture happening, we have more options to combat it. This belief is paired with another central concern: recent trends in identity politics seem to be supercharging, rather than restraining, elite capture. As

I discuss in chapter 4, this is even true of the politics of deference: an etiquette that asks people to pass attention, resources, and initiative to those perceived as more marginalized than themselves.

We should respond to the problems of elite capture, and the racial capitalism that enables it, not with deference politics but with *constructive* politics. A constructive approach would focus on outcome over process: the pursuit of specific goals or results, rather than mere avoidance of "complicity" in injustice or promotion of purely moral or aesthetic principles. A constructive approach fits squarely into what political theorist Michael Dawson calls "pragmatic utopianism . . . that starts where we are, but imagines where we want to be," combining a set of goals unbound by whatever passes for common sense today with a "hardheaded political realism" capable of finding the strategies and tactics needed to shift common sense and the world underneath it.[26]

When it comes to knowledge and information, a constructive politics would be concerned primarily with building institutions and campaign-relevant practices of information gathering, rather than centering specific groups of people or spokespeople who stand in for them. It would focus on accountability, rather than conformity. It would calibrate itself directly to the task of redistributing social resources and power, rather than to intermediary goals cashed out in pedestals or symbolism. It would focus on building and rebuilding rooms, not regulating traffic within and between them. It would be what political scientist Adom Getachew terms a "worldmaking" project, aimed at building and rebuilding actual structures of social connection and movement, rather than mere critique of the ones we already have.[27]

This book is for the people who want to see different outcomes—those who want a different, and better, world system than the one we have now. It is not a how-to guide. Rather, it is intended to help people who are doing the hard work of changing the world to see certain trends and traps that beset organizing—and thus help them respond to their own particular contexts more strategically. To that end, I want to give the best explanation of my perspective on the underlying problem of elite capture—and the best explanation of constructive politics as a response to it—that I can. We can work out collectively where to go from there.

The remainder of this book aims to answer some key questions about why elite capture matters and what we should do about it. Chapter 1 elaborates a more in-depth answer to the question "What is elite capture?" Chapter 2 follows up on this description, using it to make some headway in identifying where elite capture shows up in our social conditions and why. With all this as background, by chapter 3 we will be in a position to understand why deference politics—a kind of culture that builds itself around identity politics—fuels the elite capture of identity politics. I wrap things up in chapter 4 with some thoughts about an alternative approach, which I call constructive politics.

1

What Is Elite Capture?

In 1957, E. Franklin Frazier published a controversial work of sociology: *Black Bourgeoisie*. This work was, among other things, a pioneering analysis of elite capture that will help clarify the basic phenomenon.

Edward Franklin Frazier was born to James and Mary Clark Frazier in Baltimore, Maryland, in 1894. Though his father had managed to teach himself to read and write without having ever attended school, those hard-won markers of respectability won him no exemptions from the degradations of working life as a Black man in a racist society. Nevertheless, James made it a point to impress upon his children the importance of education. Throughout his time in Baltimore public schools, Edward seemed to take it to heart, graduating near the top of his high school class. The reward for his hard work was a scholarship to Howard University.[1]

After graduating from Howard with honors, Frazier turned to teaching while continuing his studies. He was an instructor at the Tuskegee Institute in Alabama and eventually became director of social work at the Atlanta School of

Social Work. There, American sociology and Black sociology were both being invented by a network of Black scholars that included W. E. B. Du Bois. While their scholarship likely influenced his later thinking, Frazier's time there was limited, as he was fired in 1927—after which he and his wife, Marie, moved to Chicago, where Frazier completed a doctorate in sociology while teaching at Fisk University. In 1943, he was hired at Howard University in Washington, DC, where he stayed until his death.[2]

Frazier was uncommonly successful, especially for a Black academic of his era. That was certainly not because he played it safe. His views on the Black family launched historic debates with fellow sociologist Melville Herskovits, and they continue to shape scholarship and policy decades later.[3] His 1927 firing from Atlanta was set in motion when of one of his articles, "The Pathology of Race Prejudice," broke a taboo: it analyzed white Southerners with the same anthropological eye so often trained on "other" peoples. It probably didn't help smooth things over that Frazier argued white Southern racism toward Black people was a kind of insanity. His article was picked up by the *Atlantic Constitution*, a local paper, and soon the Fraziers were on the receiving end of death threats.[4] Good old "cancel culture" at work.

But the controversy for which Frazier is known best would not be kicked off until thirty years later, with the publication of his 1957 sociological study of the US Black middle class, *Black Bourgeoisie.* In the book, Frazier accuses the Black middle class of being an insecure, powerless group constantly constructing a world of "make-believe" to deal with an "inferiority complex" caused by the brutal history of racial domination in the United States. It was instantly controversial. Frazier recalls in a preface to the 1962 edition that in the aftermath of the first edition, he was both applauded for his courage and threatened with violence.

At around the same time as Frazier was analyzing the Black bourgeoisie of the United States, Frantz Fanon was publishing seminal works of political philosophy in which he discussed mid-century African middle classes. Their approaches bore striking similarities. Fanon was writing during the wave of national independence movements in Asia and Africa that followed the conclusion of the Second World War—a time of possibility and political questions. The African middle classes of which he spoke were poised to become the national ruling elite of post-colonial societies. He described this bourgeoisie as an "underdeveloped middle class" that was "not engaged in production, nor in invention, nor building, nor labor" and thus doomed to actions of the "intermediary type": that is, to "keep in the running and to be part of the racket."[5]

These failures of this new post-colonial ruling class explain, in part, why Fanon suspected that it would capture, dilute, and ultimately subvert the energy of anti-imperialist struggle.[6] "National consciousness," he predicted, "instead of being the all-embracing crystallization of the innermost hopes of the whole people, instead of being the immediate and most obvious result of the mobilization of the people, will be in any case only an empty shell, a crude and fragile travesty of what it might have been."[7]

This prediction seemed to come true. The national independence movements supplanted formal colonial rule only to run headfirst into neocolonialism: a condition in which those young nations' new ruling elite were either sharply constrained by or actively colluding with the corporations and governments of the former colonial powers—and the international system they dominated.[8] African studies scholar Georges Nzongola-Ntalaja, writing in the early 1980s, just after this wave of independence movements, summed it up this way:

> The masses had hoped that their living conditions would be improved after independence, and this was in fact what these leaders promised them. But the promise was not honored after independence, for many reasons, one of which was the fact that the anticolonial struggle had masked the conflicts of interested between the petty bourgeoisie and ordinary people. These conflicts became manifest after independence when, instead of fulfilling their promises, the new rulers responded to popular demands either with more promises or with repression.[9]

Why were the Black "lumpenbourgeoisie" (as Frazier described them) of the United States and the newly ascendant African ruling classes so ineffective at improving the systems for Black people as a group? Frazier and Fanon alike focused on their intellectual and political failures.

Fanon referred to a belief among the African middle classes that they could "advantageously replace the middle class of the mother country," which he saw as "willful narcissism" and "intellectual laziness."[10] Frazier was similarly unbridled in his criticisms, and some of the most scathing were directed at the Black press, "the chief medium of communication which creates and perpetuates the world of make-believe for the black bourgeoisie." While acknowledging the contributions of Black publications like the *Chicago Defender* and early abolitionist organs like Frederick Douglass's *Paper*, Frazier nevertheless insisted that the Black press's "demand for equality for the Negro in American life is concerned primarily with opportunities which will benefit the black bourgeoisie economically and enhance the social status of the Negro." The elite in control of prominent Black media, he argued, would advance these subgroup interests seemingly without regard to the welfare of the larger group. Frazier gave as an example the celebration by Black newspapers of the election of a Black doctor to the presidency of a local affiliate of the American Medical Association, even though the doctor had opposed a national health program and the AMA itself opposed "socialized medicine."[11] Good old respectability politics at work.

A central argument of *Black Bourgeoisie* concerns a generations-old political strategy for racial uplift: the project of building a separate Black economy within the United States. Booker T. Washington's National Negro Business League, which first convened in Boston, Massachusetts, in 1900, is a classic example of this strategy, which debuted to great enthusiasm and fanfare among Black business leaders. Frazier, however, argued that Washington's approach was misguided, based on faulty analysis of the economic situation of African Americans at the time. The combined net worth of all 115 attendees at the inaugural National Negro Business League did not amount to even $1 million. By the time Frazier wrote his book, more than six decades later, all eleven Black-owned banks in the nation combined did not represent the amount of capital held in the average local bank in smaller white cities. Frazier thus concludes that an African American economy was a pipe dream all along.[12]

Not only would building a national Black economy be mathematically almost impossible, Frazier asserted; the attempt would also be politically naive. Such an economy would have to be bootstrapped out of the present political reality, which would make it vulnerable to outside influence—despite being a response to that very vulnerability. Even if people are successfully persuaded to "buy Black," Frazier argued, if they're doing so with dollars earned from their job at the Ford plant, then we haven't yet created a Black economy.

Why does the myth of a Black economy as a comprehensive response to anti-Black racism survive, even if prominent Black businesspeople have long been in a position to know that it wasn't a serious possibility? Frazier contends that it owes its persistence to the particular class interests of the small but influential Black bourgeoisie who were behind the idea. Some of these were business owners hoping to enjoy a monopoly of the African American economic market. Others were salaried professionals—far and away the largest percentage of the Black middle class in the mid-twentieth century—hoping to work their way into white-owned marketing firms on the strength of their presumed knowledge of the untapped potential of Black purchasing power in the Cold War economy.

Whether on the part of the Black press or the Black entrepreneurs, Frazier claims that "the black bourgeoisie have shown no interest in the 'liberation' of Negroes"—that is, unless "it affected their own status or acceptance by the white community."[13] Given half a chance, "the black bourgeoisie has exploited the Negro masses as ruthlessly as have whites."[14] Frazier surely overstates things here. Nonetheless, his book, like Fanon's work, offers a crisp depiction of elite capture that remains valuable.

Today, we are about as far in time from Frazier's *Black Bourgeoisie* and Fanon's *Black Skin, White Masks* as Frazier and Fanon were from Booker T. Washington's National Negro Business League. But little has changed. In his comprehensive analysis of the current state of this political trajectory, communication studies scholar Jared A. Ball reveals a set of political arrangements much like the one Frazier depicted more than a half century earlier. There have been some twists and turns: as Ball explains, the latest iteration of the mythical Black economy-to-freedom pipeline centers narrowly on African Americans' economic power as consumers rather than as bankers or as producers. According to the myth, Black Americans have over $1 trillion worth of power as consumers that they could use to bootstrap themselves into power and freedom, but instead squander on fashion and other frivolous purchases. This concept of "buying power," he argues, was developed by the US government and business elites and is maintained in implicit partnership with Black businesspeople and media elites—roughly the same cast of characters Frazier referred to as the Black "lumpenbourgeoisie."[15] Ball adds that the "buying power" variant of this myth also serves to shift focus and blame onto the supposed "financial illiteracy" of the Black poor, as opposed to the social and economic conditions that exploit, oppress, and marginalize people.[16]

Ball's analysis reiterates Frazier's: in each story, what lies behind the "movement for a Black economy" is a myth and a material reality. The possibility of an insulated Black economy is the myth, while the immediate interests of a few well-positioned Black folk provide the true impetus. And in both versions of the story, it is the problem—the institutions and patterns of the status quo—that is offered up as the solution.

Who Runs the World? Elites

Confronted with this problem that masquerades as solution, Frazier and Ball both get right something crucial that critics of "identity politics"—as well as "wokeness," "cancel culture," and many other hot-button terms—frequently get wrong. Critics and detractors of these political commitments claim that they reflect the social preoccupations of "rich white people" or the "professional-managerial class." And they're not completely wrong. But that fact is just something that identity politics, wokeness, and the like have in common with *everything else* in our lives: the increasing domination of elite interests and control over aspects of our social system. That's because almost everything in our social world has a tendency to fall prey to elite capture. In other words, it's not just that wokeness is too white. It's that *everything* is.

True, whiteness and eliteness are two very different things. For our purposes, though, this is a fair dig because they have gone hand in hand in many parts of the world for the past few hundred years, with consequences that have shaped everything around us.

The core concern of this book is eliteness as such—and there's no hard and fast rule about what kind of person can be an elite. Sometimes you're an elite because of how people have decided (or been forced) to relate to some aspect of your social identity. Sometimes you're an elite because of some more contingent advantage: your level of education, wealth, or social prestige. Sometimes you're an elite just because you happen to be the only one of your group who's in a particular room. According to political scientist Jo Freeman, "an elite refers to a small group of people who have power over a larger group of which they are part, usually without direct responsibility to that larger group, and often without their knowledge or consent."[17] You'll notice that Freeman doesn't treat the status of "elite" as a stable identity—it's a relationship, in a particular context, between a smaller group of people and a larger group of people.

Elite capture happens when the advantaged few steer resources and institutions that could serve the many toward their own narrower interests and aims. The term is used in economics, political science, and related disciplines to describe the way socially advantaged people tend to gain control over benefits meant for everyone.[18] In this context, it has been used

much like the more familiar label of "corruption" and identified by similar symptoms of undue influence, such as bribes.[19]
But the concept has also been applied to describe how political projects more generally can be hijacked—in principle or in
effect—by the well positioned and better resourced.

As economist Diya Dutta explains, elite capture, in es-
sence, refers to "the presence of unequal access to power—
some have greater access to power (by virtue of their lineage,
or caste, or economic wealth or gender or some other reason) and consequently the ability to influence the transfer
of funds/resources disproportionately."[20] Public goods and
resources such as knowledge, attention, and values are unfairly distributed, just as much as material wealth and political power are. More precisely, the distribution patterns of all
these are distorted in similar ways, for similar reasons. Elite
capture is symptomatic of social systems with unequal bal-
ances of power.

Does Democracy Matter?

If liberal political theory offered an accurate view of the
world (which it doesn't), then one might conclude that the
balance of power in many areas of the world is already okay.
Many places in the world are self-proclaimed democracies,
after all, and the democratic system is supposed to be all
about a healthy balance of power. In democracies, ostensi-
bly, the elites (policymakers) are put in office by the non-
elites (citizens), who can remove and replace them if they fail

to defend public interests. Much like the mythical market, mythical liberal democracy is supposed to be self-correcting and self-justifying by definition. This way of casting the conversation about power and governance has been integral to the framing that links "freedom" and "capitalism" in the ideals and practices of liberal democracy: a country's freedom need only be found at its ballot boxes rather than in, say, its workplaces.[21] Thus, if one believes in liberal democracy, they may believe that imbalances of power everywhere could be fixed by instituting arrangements like the "rules-based international order," "democratic elections," and "formal political representation." In a nutshell, if the right ideals are embodied in the right formal systems, then the outcomes of those systems are justified.

To be clear, formal arrangements *do* matter. Phrases like "formal political representation" are genuinely meaningful, given that places with less formal political representation *do* tend to operate differently than places with more. But these phrases get bandied about in ways that are often less than meaningful. So if we want to hang our hopes on the ideals of democratic accountability, we should take stock of how far we are from actually achieving even this low bar for control over our own lives. After decades of this liberal democratic rhetoric, actual decision-making structures rarely rely on actual democratic accountability.

We are likeliest to talk about elite capture at the national level. In her book *From #BlackLivesMatter to Black Liberation*, Princeton professor Keeanga-Yamahtta Taylor cites the telling example of the Congressional Black Caucus's cosponsorship of

Ronald Reagan's 1986 Anti–Drug Abuse Act, which helped supercharge mass incarceration by establishing mandatory minimum sentencing guidelines and adding $1.7 billion toward the drug war, while welfare programs were cut.[22] This legislation solved a problem for the Reaganites and the Black elites of the Congressional Black Caucus alike, allowing them to look busy with respect to the crack cocaine epidemic. But with the law's passage, working-class African Americans went from dealing with one very complex problem to weathering two interlocking ones: the drug epidemic itself—unsolved by this draconian measure—and the surge of discriminatory law enforcement the legislation unleashed. These consequences led Democratic senator Daniel Patrick Moynihan to make a striking appraisal: "If we blame crime on crack, our politicians are off the hook. Forgotten are failed schools, the malign welfare programs, the desolate neighborhoods, the wasted years. Only crack is to blame. One is tempted to think that if crack did not exist, someone somewhere would have received a federal grant to develop it."[23]

It is often alleged that the federal government was directly responsible for the crack epidemic.[24] However, not much hinges on whether there was an active conspiracy. For a combination of laziness, callous indifference, and opportunism was perfectly sufficient: the elites at the levers of funding and oversight saw what was in their own best interest and then simply did that; its foreseeable negative effects on those they supposedly represent weren't an effective deterrent.

And then there's capital. The 1950s and 60s saw important innovations in corporate management (particularly in the

United States, which stood comfortably atop the post-World War II global economy): leveraged buyouts, divestitures, mergers, major sell-offs of "non-core-businesses," and other forms of reorganization of businesses by profit-hungry shareholders.[25] These trends intensified in the 1980s, producing what researchers call the "shareholder revolution": a proliferation of management techniques that put previously complacent industry managers under the strict discipline of activist shareholders.[26] This second phase of shareholder revolution coincided with and helped produce a larger "global business revolution," a "fast-developing process of concentration at a global level in numerous industries supplying goods and services" to "systems integrators"—the few large firms who can reorganize global production around their "core" business model and assets.[27]

The elites atop "system integrator" mega-corporations have not stopped at reorganizing global production around their pursuit of shareholder value. In fact, they are reorganizing everything. Corporations have built their own shadow court system of "arbitration," effectively removing entire industries from even the barest pretense of judicial review.[28] Public service projects across the world, but especially in the global South, have been financed by "public-private partnerships": "long-term contractual arrangements through which the private sector commits to finance and manage public services . . . as long as the state shares the risks." Economists Ndongo Samba Sylla and Daniela Gabor explain that this has functioned in ways characteristic of racial capitalism: building financial security for shareholders by way of financial and other forms of precarity for the people in countries like Senegal and the Ivory Coast who are charged high user fees to access privately financed infrastructure.[29] Making matters worse, social media tech giants own huge swaths of the world's attention economy, running platforms that are rife with abuse—a 2021 investigation by journalist Karen Hao found that the largest Facebook pages targeting "Christian Americans" and "African Americans" were run by troll farms exploiting Facebook algorithms to send information to tens of millions of Americans with the aim of inflaming and exploiting social divisions. These farms also operate in India, the United Kingdom, and throughout Central and South America.[30]

But elite capture is perhaps clearest at the multinational level, where weighty decisions about economic possibilities are made by large global institutions without even the pretense of democratic accountability. These institutions emerged as the world order was being reconstructed in the waning years of the Second World War, with the United States newly emergent as a global hegemon. The architects met in Bretton Woods, New Hampshire, where they set up the International Monetary Fund (IMF) and what later became the World Bank. Whatever the narrow "technical" pretensions of their mandates, these organizations in fact have immense governing power. They offer aid packages that are conditional on certain governance decisions by the receiving country—decisions that help determine the availability of jobs, public services, and the price of food. These basic features of non-elite life are thus placed in the hands of foreign bureaucrats over whom the country's population have no means of democratic control, nor even the pretense of any sort of democratic relationship.[31]

The 1980s featured a particularly controversial set of "structural adjustment programs" through which the IMF strong-armed governments into liberalizing markets and devaluing currency in order to qualify for needed loans.[32] And why did they need the loans badly enough to take such a deal? Broadly, because colonial governments had expropriated so much value from the colonies, in a myriad of ways, for centuries. The World Bank and IMF continue to encourage post-colonial nations to maintain high levels of predatorily securitized debt today. By maintaining financial control, they operate as de facto governing bodies, tying needed aid to politically distorting conditions.[33]

The control exerted by these Bretton Woods institutions lacks even the aesthetic of democracy. Since voting power is allocated by measures of wealth rather than population, middle- and low-income countries (much of the global South) have a minority share of votes despite making up 85 percent of the world's population.[34] The process of voting in these institutions is thus skewed in the direction of yesterday's power blocs, rather than today's needs. Moreover, the heads of the World Bank and IMF are typically from the United States and Europe and are nominated by these states, not elected in any sense (even a skewed one).

There have been genuine attempts to defy the World Bank and IMF. For decades, Latin Americans have elected populist leaders in response to the most recent developments in neoliberal capitalism. But the results have been mixed, and the failures have been bloody. Ecuador, for example, has experienced decades of conflict between "radical resource nationalists" and "anti-extractivists," a debate that was made possible (if not inevitable) by the country's dependence on fossil fuel extraction for the revenue that funds its social projects and services its sovereign debt.[35]

Over the decades between the Second World War and the present, the functional partnership between capitalism and liberal democracy, with its semblance of popular legitimacy, has weakened across the globe. It is for this reason that legal scholar Issa Shivji describes liberal democracy as being "under siege." In his view, it is in decline because of the sociological traps set by monopoly capitalism: "jobless growth, inequitable distribution, and unbearable inequality," and the resulting alienation of much of the population from the political system.[36] Similarly, sociologist Wolfgang Streeck argues that the liberal democratic ideal has been disintegrating for decades. Rather than a cataclysmic putsch or violent event, for Streeck, the end of democracy simply *is* the gradual capture of the political by the elites: "[A]s one crisis followed the next, and the fiscal crisis of the state unfolded alongside them, the arena of distributional conflict shifted, moving upwards and away from the world of collective action of citizens towards ever more remote decision sites where interests appear as 'problems' in the abstract jargon of technocratic specialists."[37]

Capture at Every Scale

Streeck describes some common features of elite capture: less collective action by people, more remote decision sites, and the rise of technocrats. Such shifts are visible not only at the level of national and international policy, but at smaller levels of organization as well.

Take, for example, the section of the world where I work: the ivory tower. In *Philosophy of African American Studies*, North Carolina State University professor Stephen Ferguson II describes the elite capture of Black studies, which owes its existence to the radical student movements of the 1960s and '70s but has since been "turned into a bureaucratic cog in the academic wheel controlled by administrators, with virtually no democratic input from students or the Black working-class community."[38]

This is not a special feature of the ivory tower's influence on Black politics. The Combahee River Collective formed in part because of failures of solidarity across several overlapping axes of difference: gender lines within Black liberation struggles, racial lines within women's liberation movements, and sexuality lines within Black feminist organizations. Neither these tensions nor the forms of elite capture they represent were new in their day: Angela Davis's *Women, Race, and Class* presents a masterful analysis of similar forms of capture by the best positioned feminists during the anti-slavery and early women's rights movements of the nineteenth century.[39] Some scholars argue that E. Franklin Frazier himself exemplified some of these tendencies, tying social problems in the

Black community too closely with the prevalence of women-headed households.[40]

Or, instead of broadening the context we look for elite capture within, we could maintain the same scale but reverse the identities. That is: instead of thinking about the class politics of racial studies, one could describe the race politics of class activism, where we might find that whites (racial elites) tend to capture the decision-making process of socialist organizations, labor unions, and the like.[41]

Elite capture is not particular to Black politics. Take, for example, the last few decades of queer politics, illustrated in the aptly titled essay "You Wanted Same-Sex Marriage? Now You Have Pete Buttigieg." *BuzzFeed* writer Shannon Keating laments the gradual trajectory of mainstream queer politics away from the more radical and progressive elements dramatized by the 1969 Stonewall riots and the confrontational organizing of New York's AIDS Coalition to Unleash Power (ACT UP), toward assimilationist goals of being represented by, and treated like, Democratic politicians such as Buttigieg—telegenic, monogamous, white, financially secure, and vocally Christian. As Keating says, "The best way for queer people to get ahead, it seems, is still to act as though we are *just like everybody else*."[42] Barbara Smith, one of the original organizers of the Combahee River Collective (who, as described in chapter 1, came up with the term "identity politics"), left active involvement in the mainstream LGBTQ movement for this reason.[43]

When we look at uneven distributions of power, at every scale, in every context, the patterns of elite capture eventually show up. In the absence of the right kind of checks or constraints, the subgroup of people with power over and access to the resources used to describe, define, and create political realities—in other words, the elites—will capture the group's values, forcing people to coordinate on a narrower social project that disproportionately represents elite interests. When elites run the show, the interests of the group get whittled down to what they have in common with those at the top, at best. At worst, elites fight for their own narrow interests using the banner of group solidarity.

This chapter has tried to make good on something I claim in the introduction: that elite capture is a general political problem, not a special one faced by antiracist or identity politics alone. Noticing *that* elite capture shows up across our global social system is a good start. But if we are going to do something about it, it would also help to know *why*.

2

Reading the Room

Anne Eliza Riddle was in an uncommon position. Maybe her mistress was just unusually enthusiastic about reading. Or perhaps it had something to do with the fact that Anna was unusually fair skinned—rumor had it that one of her grandfathers was white. In which case Anna's mistress might well have also been Anna's aunt. Either way, her mistress broke the law, and so Anna was put in the uncommon position of being an enslaved Black person who knew how to read.

Whatever the merits of this small kindness by the planter family, it was overshadowed by the harsh realities of racial slavery, including the fact that they responded to financial difficulties in Anna's adolescence by threatening to sell her mother and two youngest brothers. Heroically, the teenaged Anna offered herself on the auction block to keep the rest of her family together. But she didn't fetch high-enough bids, so the planter family reverted to the original plan, tragically breaking up their family.[1]

A few years later, during the US Civil War, James Henry Woodson also found himself in an uncommon position in

Confederate territory. James was on the run. His owner had loaned him and his labor to a man who put him to work digging ditches, but James had used his spare time to make traps and furniture to sell and make money for himself. One day, the man found James working on precisely this. Furious at this affront, he tried to whip James—but James, knowing that the Union Army was nearby, hit him back and fled to his owner's house. He explained the situation as a "falling out," which to his aggravated owner sounded like a symptom of a much bigger problem. "Fell out! That's the trouble now! All free! All free," the white man exclaimed. And James replied, "Yes, we are free. . . . And if you bother me, I'll kill you, another devil." And off he went again.[2]

But James did not simply run *away* from the white planter he had threatened; he turned east, toward Richmond, Virginia, where he'd heard he could find Union soldiers. James did indeed meet some soldiers, and he told them his story. He led them first to the man who had so recently tried to whip him, and the soldiers "punished" the planter. Then James took them to various Confederate supply stations and warehouses, helping the Union to ransack the Southern army's supplies. He spent the rest of the Civil War scouting for the Union Army in much the same way. In so doing, James joined the ranks of the many enslaved African Americans who engaged in sabotage, withdrew their labor, and fought militarily—the "general strike," in the words of W. E. B. Du Bois, that helped defeat the Confederacy and destroy the system of racial slavery.[3]

Anna and James married shortly after the war, in 1867. The iron-willed couple tried their hand at the deeply rigged game of sharecropping, managing to scrape together enough money to buy a small farm in West Virginia. There, in 1875, they had their fourth child: Carter Godwin Woodson. Farm life was hard work, requiring the efforts of the entire family, but Anna made sure Carter and his siblings also received an education. They spent four months of the year in a one-room schoolhouse run by two of Anna's brothers who had also learned to read. This meant that Carter was both the child and student of former slaves.[4]

When Carter was seventeen, he found a job working in the coal mines of West Virginia. When one of his coworkers, a Black Civil War veteran, found out that Carter could read, the Black miners hatched a plan: they would pool their money to subscribe to the African American run *Richmond Planet* as well as several white daily newspapers, and Carter would read the papers aloud to the group. These reading and discussion groups helped Carter learn more and more about the wider world.

But he didn't stop there. Carter breezed through four years' worth of high school courses in two and took college courses at Berea, a rare racially integrated college in Kentucky founded by the abolitionist John Fee in 1855—all while serving, first, as an instructor at a school for miners' children, then, as principal of a school for African Americans.[5] After winning the Spanish–American War of 1898, the United States took over colonial possession of the Philippines from the Spanish—affording Carter, a US citizen, the opportunity to make a decent salary in the new colony teaching English and farming by day, while learning Spanish, French, and European history by night.

Using this knowledge and savings, Carter traveled throughout Asia, Africa, and Europe, learning about their education systems and attending lectures on the history of different places as he went. He returned to the United States in 1907 determined to become a scholar and correct history's silence about Black people: both the racist exclusion of African Americans from US history and widespread ignorance of and disinterest in African history.[6] After picking up a second undergraduate degree and a master's degree at the University of Chicago, he enrolled at Harvard University, where he earned a PhD in history. He was only the second African American to do so, after W. E. B. Du Bois.[7]

Despite having a PhD, Woodson was not destined for a steady life in academia. He was uncompromising in his standards, which put him at odds with many of the people who may have otherwise helped his academic career. In 1919, freshly arrived at Howard University, he created the university's first African American history course; the very next year, he came under the scrutiny of the administration for criticizing his employer in a major newspaper. This was the height of the Red Scare—the Russian Revolution of 1917 had just panicked elites the world over—and Senator Reed Smoot had criticized the university for having in its library a pamphlet on "the Bolsheviks and the Soviets."[8] When Howard's president ordered the item pulled from the collection, Carter couldn't keep quiet, and he soon found himself without a job.

But employed as such or not, Carter G. Woodson remained a scholar. He had already founded the *Journal of Negro History*, through which he continued his pioneering work in African American history by producing scholarship to his own exacting standard, and supporting young and emerging scholars, including Zora Neale Hurston. He also founded the Association for the Study of Negro Life and History (today known as the Association for the Study of African American Life and History), supported by a grassroots fundraising effort. Through Negro history clubs in high schools, theatrical renditions of historical events, and posters, the organization spread knowledge of Black history across the country.[9] His books were among those secretly used by Black educators nationwide to subvert white control over what Black schoolchildren learned. All of these efforts contributed to the broader network of intellectually insurgent practices of Black scholars and educators that education scholar Jarvis Givens calls "fugitive pedagogy."[10]

According to Howard University historian Daryl Michael Scott, Woodson believed that publishing "scientific history" would transform race relations. Scott points out that during the civil rights movement a few years later, Carter's approach to history was taught in the Freedom Schools that organizers set up across the South. "The Negro History movement," he explains, "was an intellectual insurgency that was part of every larger effort to transform race relations."[11]

But why did Carter think that an intellectual movement could seriously challenge a political structure?

Carter G. Woodson was a historian, and he was arguably a philosopher as well. This is apparent in much of his work, but especially in the 1933 book *The Mis-Education of the Negro*, in which he explains how elite capture structures societies' education systems. Woodson's keen insights provide a blueprint for a more general process that occurs at many levels and in many contexts throughout our social lives.

In the previous chapter, I noted the astonishing extent of elite capture: how many of our institutions, resources, and even political agendas evidence the direct control or significantly disproportionate influence of the most advantaged among us. But I haven't yet described, in a rich and textured sense, what elite capture *is*, at bottom. Understanding this might help explain why elite capture shows up in so many different parts of human social life, from the education system to the housing market; from the small-scale internal dynamics of an activist group to the massive scale of a government. But more importantly, understanding what elite capture is could help us identify it when we see it—and having identified it, to at least plot strategies to curb its worst excesses in our movements and in our own lives.

A trip through a fairy tale, accompanied by some philosophers and game theorists, will help us clarify what elite capture is—and why we see it everywhere we turn.

The Ground We Stand On

You've no doubt heard the story of the emperor who had no clothes. As Hans Christian Andersen told it, functionaries of the emperor handed him a hanger, claiming that it held a garment made of a mystical fabric that would appear invisible to anyone incompetent or exceptionally stupid. In fact, the hanger held nothing at all. The emperor put on the "garment" and walked around the town naked. Having heard of the myth claiming that, to point out the obvious, nakedness would confirm one's own incompetence and unintelligence, none of his subjects dared to point out the obvious—not even the servant assigned to hold the "train" of his nonexistent garment. The spell holds even as the emperor is escorted through the town in a celebratory parade. Finally, a young child yells: "But he hasn't got anything on." The spell is broken.

Like most fables, this story encapsulates deep insights about the social world. One insight is about how our interactions with each other are fundamentally structured by power. It's tempting to explain our oppressive social hierarchies and structures in terms of our sincere commitments: our beliefs, attitudes, and tightly held ideologies. When we look at things this way, we see racism as a way of thinking about one's place in the world (as "supreme," as "human") and a set of beliefs about others' place, misogyny as a way of looking at the masculine and the feminine (aggrandizing the former, disrespecting the latter), and so on.

This way of understanding phenomena in terms of ideology or belief has merit: surely what we genuinely believe about ourselves, what this world is like, and what we owe to each other all *affects* how we move through the world. But the relationship between what each of us takes to be true and good, and how we manage our specific day-to-day interactions is a lot more tenuous than this approach suggests, which is one of the insights that the story of the naked emperor seems tailor-made to share with us.

The interaction between the emperor and the crowd is one illustration of how as we talk or interact, we build the world together. Words, gestures, and signs don't interpret themselves; it's up to their users and observers to make something out of them. Communication is a kind of "joint action" in which each individual is playing their part in a thing *we're* doing together.[12] Accordingly, philosophers of language have often emphasized that we have to share to communicate. Among these things we share is information: after all, if we had to start from scratch, constructing our basic picture of the world every time we started a conversation, it would be hard to ever talk about anything interesting or do anything remotely complicated together. Instead, when we communicate, we presume certain "common beliefs" or "mutual beliefs"—not just things that *I* know and that *you* know, but things I-know-that-you-know, you-know-that-I-know, and so on.[13]

Philosopher Robert Stalnaker calls this public information the "common ground," likening it to a shared resource that participants in a conversation use to build and perform social interactions.[14] As we move through the world, the "ground" shifts beneath us. We add things to the common ground when we share information and perspectives. Our collective responses to events happening around us create new common ground over time. And we change the common ground when we use our words to challenge and reshape it, from defying personal rumors to renewing long-held cultural wisdom. Each of these interactions changes what information we treat as public and shared.

What's important about this public information is what we do with it. When we act in social contexts, we treat the information in the common ground *as if it were true*: that is, we treat it as a premise for public action.[15] Use of this common bank of assumptions is ubiquitous in social life: its because we share so many assumptions about meals and socializing that my partner telling me that friends are coming over tonight suffices to get me to cook more food and set extra places at the dinner table. Similarly, the townsfolk in the fable treat a naked emperor, presumed clothed, as the premise of their shared activity of cheering. And this makes sense of their choice to cheer, at one level. But, as the fable's setting dramatizes, there are all kinds of reasons to act as if something is true.[16] Genuine belief is just one potential reason among many.

The rise of social media has made us hyperaware of something that has always been true about communication: the social world in which we talk to each other is complex, and what we want out of interactions often goes far beyond what we're saying on the surface. We aim to manage relationships and reputations; to pursue clout or to frustrate someone else's attempt to do the same; to bolster our "side" of disputes that are political (in senses both grand and small); to gain resources and rewards or to avoid punishments and obstacles.

Much like common sense, common ground isn't always quite as "common" as advertised. On a good day, we communicate in good faith and for good reasons. Maybe we accept a new idea that challenges our previous perspective and incorporate it into our sense of the common. We do that as part of meaningfully sharing the world with the people around us, trusting that they too communicate in good faith and for good reasons.

We may accept new information into the common ground because we believe this information to be true, and reject old information because we believe it to be false—certainly this is the way the scientists of the world would like things to proceed—and we care about tending to the quality of our common ground to the extent that our ability to live and flourish together depends on it. This, at least, is a picture of the way that the common ground might work in a social context in which we distribute trust, respect, and authority in just and fair ways, and where we communicate in ways that seek the common good. Sounds nice, doesn't it?

Our social contexts are, of course, much less rosy than that.

Consider a different scenario. This one comes from the philosopher of language David Lewis.[17] Lewis, true to the detached style of so-called analytic philosophers, introduces the example as a dry, bloodless thought experiment: "For some reason—coercion, deference, common purpose—two people are both willing that one of them should be under the control of the other. (At least within certain limits, in a certain sphere of action, so long as certain conditions prevail.) Call one the *slave*, the other the *master*. The control is exercised verbally, as follows."[18] But this framing is deceptive. Since slavery was an actual social institution, Lewis is in effect describing rules of communication that governed actual interactions that were part and parcel of the construction of racial capitalism and the global political system it produced.

Still, let's stay with this bloodless thought experiment for just a moment. A master speaking to their slave occupies a position of power that decides what is communicatively possible when they interact. For example, their refusal to consider the possibility that it is raining outside rules out ways of speaking that presume that it is raining. It is in the nature of their social relationship—and, as a result, of their conversations—that this power relationship only goes one way. The slave's experience of the rain, however direct, is not eligible to contribute to shared understandings. The common ground is not a democratically governed resource, for the same reason none of the other resources around them are: they live in a slave society.

Communication is often described in overly intellectual terms that take its role as information exchange a bit too seriously. On such views, to have one's offer of public information unfairly rejected is to be harmed in some special "epistemic" way "as a knower."[19] The systems of injustice that show up in our communicative interactions are then frequently treated as a special ideological kind of injustice, rooted in a belief system that stands apart from or even behind other systems of injustice.[20]

But another possibility is that communication is simply a kind of action, and thus that the way we act in conversation is largely governed by the exact same forces, norms, and incentives that explain everything else we do. Elites "capture" our conversations, then, for largely the same reasons and in the same ways as they capture everything else.

What are the townspeople who cheer the naked emperor thinking? We could, if we wanted to, build an intricate intellectual architecture to explain why the townspeople cheer. We could imagine that they are true believers, with a whole complex of legitimizing myths. Maybe both the emperor and the townspeople are genuinely persuaded by the false story of the invisible garment because they believe *another* false story about the emperor's unique insight into the deep structure of reality, or because they believe in some supernatural mechanism that punishes personal faults with hallucinations. This is the kind of explanation that people often give when they try to explain oppression by appeal to "implicit bias," "ideology," "epistemic injustice," or cultural explanations rooted in the moral and spiritual rot of oppressive societies.

Something is wrong with *the townspeople themselves*, these explanations seem to say. So, if we want to know why the townspeople are behaving this strange way on this strange day, we had better figure out what ails them psychologically or culturally, or in some other dimension that shapes their perceptions and intuitions. Surely those who adopt this perspective are onto *something*. It would be hard to imagine that a society could demand slavish conversational obedience across days, years, and generations without any ramifications whatsoever on how people actually think and feel about the world, and act in it.

But we get a different answer if we ask not why the townspeople *believe* the emperor, but rather why they are acting *as if* they believe the emperor. Put another way, from this perspective it is not *beliefs* that are being systematically organized, but *behavior.* This way of thinking about the situation still allows the possibility that the townspeople in fact hold belief structures that inform their behavior. But unlike the first approach, it concerns itself seriously with what's in it for the townsfolk if they play along—and what's at stake for them if they do not.

If people make communicative decisions for the same kinds of reasons that they take other actions, then the whole situation becomes much less mysterious. The question of what all those townspeople cheering the naked emperor were thinking might simply and plausibly be: "If I don't play along with the emperor, something bad might happen to me."

This adjustment might seem slight, but it clarifies one reason to be dissatisfied with the kinds of explanations that involve beliefs and attitudes and culture: in taking the formal justifications for hierarchical interactions a little too seriously, they risk deeply misunderstanding what's really happening between people, especially when it comes to abusive interactions. Robin D. G. Kelley and James C. Scott have convincingly argued that even their fellow professional historians are prone to this sort of error, in their tendency to mistake broad swaths of history during which oppressed populations have "played along" with oppressive systems for evidence that they were "true believers" in those systems.[21] Indeed, some of them were as far from true believers as you can imagine: tricksters playing along with a social script even while they craftily resisted the powers that be.[22]

We don't have to assume that the baker and candlestick maker, who the naked emperor passes on the street as they are just trying to get through their days, have any interest at all in the question of whether or not the emperor is, in fact, clothed. We could guess that their guiding interests are in selling that day's bread and candles—that is, in keeping food on the table and tax collectors off their back. Standing behind their immediate state of mind as they watch the emperor come into view will be personal histories and pieces of common ground. Perhaps both citizens know the fairy tale of the commoner who becomes a nobleman because the emperor is so delighted with his wares. Or they might have in the back of their minds the much more probable, even mundane story of a businessman imprisoned or publicly tortured for unpaid debts or insulting the imperial throne.

There are many possible backstories that could lead a baker and a candlestick maker to set up shop on a street the emperor sometimes parades down, and that could shape their thoughts as they see him approach, and not one of them is about what the emperor is or isn't wearing—nor about what the baker or candlestick maker really believes about what the emperor is wearing. Yet it turns out that these kinds of stories do an adequate job all on their own of explaining why a baker and candlestick maker might play along with whatever an emperor expects them to do that day.

All it takes to understand this story is to stare patiently at what authority *is* and how it functions to organize social life.

The problem, it turns out, isn't the emperor's townspeople at all, or even the emperor. It's the *town*. It's the empire.

The Theory of Miseducation

Enough with the metaphors. The point is clear enough, when simply stated: our political structures affect the structure of all of our interactions.[23] This is the point that Carter G. Woodson's travels throughout the world made to him very powerfully, and because his analysis remains so potent, we're going to dive into it a little further.

One of Woodson's critiques is more or less about Black political strategy. The "so-called modern education" being provided to Black students, Woodson felt, was rather like the "special systems set up by private agencies and governments to educate the natives in their colonies and dependencies" and "worked out in conformity to the needs of those who have enslaved and oppressed weaker peoples."[24] It was meant to confer diplomas and other markers of social prestige and distinction to select groups of African Americans, for whom removal from the rest of the Black community was generally both the reward and the cost. As a program of "racial uplift," he said, this amounted to an attempt to transform Black people *themselves* in the image of an oppressive society. A better mission would be to change the social conditions of their oppression.

His second critique, concerning the content of the education available to Blacks, further connects the dots. Woodson pointed out that the curricula being taught were all built around information selected as important by the dominant racist education system. He provides a memorable example in the third chapter of *Mis-Education*:

> In medical schools Negroes were likewise convinced of their inferiority in being reminded of their role as germ carriers. The prevalence of syphilis and tuberculosis among Negroes was especially emphasized without showing that these maladies are more deadly among the Negroes for the reason that they are Caucasian dis-

eases; and since these plagues are new to Negroes, these sufferers have not had time to develop against them the immunity which time has permitted in the Caucasian. Other diseases to which Negroes easily fall prey were mentioned to point out the race as an undesirable element when this condition was due to the Negroes' economic and social status. Little emphasis was placed upon the immunity of the Negro from diseases like yellow fever and influenza which are so disastrous to whites. Yet, the whites were not considered inferior because of this differential resistance to these plagues.[25]

Woodson's description refers to teachers' reports of medical information about African American populations. He doesn't dispute the numbers—the teachers were adding *accurate* information into the common ground. Nevertheless, Woodson contends, this information served to support racism. That's because of what was in the common ground already: a picture of the world in which statistical information about diseases prevalent among Black people fit naturally into prevailing and preexisting narratives about their uncleanliness and inferiority, whereas equivalent information about diseases disproportionately prevalent among whites fit into preexisting narratives around their superiority. The racism was not necessarily embedded in this particular sentence, this particular instance of communication, but in the narrative in which it was embedded.

Woodson paints a vivid picture of how the background system of power structures classroom interactions in ways that are complex—but also, if we're being real, well understood.

It's exactly the same dynamics that assure the naked emperor he can count on fawning compliments about his robe. There is no balanced reporting, no symmetrical communication possible in an imperial classroom. That asymmetry in education was a product, and Woodson knew it—he had studied in the halls where it was produced.

Carter G. Woodson's first understanding of how power shapes history came early. As a young coal miner in West Virginia, he had spent years learning about the Civil War from people who had actually fought in it. This education included animated debates between coworkers at the railroad yard where his father, James, worked alongside many former Confederates—debates that their employer put an end to after an argument between James and his ex-Confederate foreman came to blows.

Later, as a graduate student at Harvard University, Woodson studied under towering historians like Edward Channing, who would go on to win the Pulitzer Prize. Channing argued in his seminar not only that African Americans had no distinctive history, but also that they had had no important role in major historical events, including the US Civil War. Woodson pushed back against his professor, who challenged him to prove his point of view. Little did Channing know, his student's intention to do just that was a major reason he was studying at Harvard in the first place. Indeed, Carter was already well aware that the textbooks citing men like Channing coddled and elevated the perspectives that empowered people like James Woodson's foreman, and ignored the perspective of those like James.

These experiences inspired Woodson to produce a different kind of history: African American history. Through the *Journal of Negro History*, and the educational institutions he founded, he went on to produce a Black history that met his own exacting academic standards.

The point was not just to change hearts and minds, but to change the *common ground*—to change what information was *usable* by people in their daily interactions.

Elite Capture: Game It Out

In *Mis-Education*, Carter shares a number of valuable insights into the nature of communication, politics, history, and education, and this book will not do justice to all of them. Most pressing, for our purposes, are his insights into the political philosophy of language, as they help us get very close to understanding elite capture. And they yield even more insight when placed in conversation with another area of philosophy that also thinks about our interactions with each other in structured environments: namely, the philosophy of games.

In *Games: Agency as Art*, philosopher C. Thi Nguyen explains the key differences between *game worlds* and *real worlds*, and what we can learn about the second from the first.[26] Games have lower stakes: if my character "dies," if I fall behind in the Mario Kart race, we can just turn the console off and start over. They also feature an artificially clear decision-making environment: I know exactly what my goals should be and how to relate to others. Say, for example, that we're playing basketball. If they are wearing the same jersey that I'm wearing, then I help them score points, or score them myself; if they're wearing the other jersey, I try to stop them. The low stakes of games allow us to immerse ourselves in a world of make-believe where everything we do has a clear and instrumental relationship to our success.

This clear and instrumental relationship is one of the important ways that games fail to capture the complications and precarities of daily life—and doubtless part of why they make such great escapes. Our interactions with our young children, adult siblings, and aging parents are often fraught with complicated practical, psychic, and moral risks. Looming behind our everyday interactions with bosses and coworkers is the threat of failure, even joblessness (especially frightening in the United States, where joblessness carries the additional risks of houselessness and lack of health care). These high stakes would be easier to manage, perhaps, if it were just a little clearer how to play them—if there were one definitive parenting book, if you could "Neutralize Your Abusive Boss with One Weird Trick." Instead, we have to balance our own goals and needs with guesses we make about others' goals and needs, often hastily, and generally with little feedback along the way about how well we've done—except when the consequences of our mistakes speak for themselves.

The artificial clarity of game worlds is an important part of what makes them fun. Game designers build environments that give players clearer reasons to take specific actions, and the satisfaction of knowing that each action contributes to success or failure. While the clarity and simplicity of games distinguish them from our non-game experiences, that feeling that every move you make is crucial to your overall strategy of survival isn't entirely different from what occurs in actual life. As we saw in the case of the baker and the candlestick maker, power structures, like fictional environments, give people reasons to *play along*.

The potential overlap between this feature of many games and features of actual social environments is at the core of a real-world process that Nguyen describes as "value capture." Value capture is a process by which we begin with rich and subtle values, encounter simplified versions of them in the social wild, and revise our values in the direction of simplicity—thus rendering them inadequate. This kind of process is always a possible result of social interaction, but the distortions to our values are sharpest in social systems and environments where this simplicity is built into the structures of reward and punishment.

Capitalism itself is such a system: it rewards the relentless and single-minded pursuit of profit and growth—extremely narrow value systems that exclude much of what makes life worth living. But societies organized around fundamentalisms (whether religious or secular) and war have resulted in similarly warped value systems long before capitalism arrived on the scene.

In real life, the value capture process is sometimes deliberately managed by elites to manipulate and control others with game design–like tactics. Gig economy platforms like Uber and Lyft use "badges" and rating systems to manage the decision-making environment of their driver employees.[27] Even outside of work, social media features such as likes, shares, and retweets play the role of points in games. Over time, these simple metrics threaten to distort or take the place of values (say, the wish to meaningfully contribute to discussion or to take pride in the quality of one's work) that might otherwise have inflected our behavior on these platforms.

What unites these different stories is the nature of the value capture process itself. The employee who wants to do a good job may start out with complex motivations—for example, working hard while staying safe and conserving enough of their physical and emotional energy for themselves and their loved ones. Under pressure from the game-inspired environment created by her boss, however, the worker must focus on winning the tokens that communicate success to that boss, ultimately replacing the worker's initial value structure at the cost of the things it protected. For example, Disney and Amazon use obsessive "real-time worker productivity tracking" to induce employees to compete in a ratings system based on speed or volume of production.[28] Productivity and profits increase, but so do fatigue, stress, and injuries for workers, undermining their original vision of a "good job."

Perhaps the workers believe in the rating system and internalize the values to which they imagine it responds—punctuality, stamina, attention to detail. Perhaps they see and judge themselves and others by the game metrics. Or perhaps they see the emperor's ass quite clearly—but change their behavior anyway because their livelihoods depend on it. Either way, the result is a tale as old as time: the boss gains, and the worker loses.

It is clear that the forces of capital have found uses for game thinking. But, as Nguyen is careful to point out, a shadowy cabal of plotters' deliberate use of game design strategies to control people is the exception, not the rule, of value capture.[29] Deliberate or calculated intervention is not a prerequisite for value capture; rather, it requires only an environment or incentive structure that encourages excess value clarity.

For example, we can imagine ourselves participating in good faith conversations on a new social media platform about a particular social issue. This platform is structured, of course, by designers employed by the company owners, who build and manage algorithms that direct the traffic of posts and encourage consumer engagement. As we talk on this platform, its features begin to affect our behavior: simpler takes attract comments and shares, affecting what people say on the platform. The tech-company owners get the lion's share of revenue generated by the site's traffic, driven by our conversations, and a small number of site participants get the lion's share of attention directed by the activity on the platform. An elite emerges.

It would be a mistake, however, to understand everything that happens on the platform as a process orchestrated by the elites. They are its *results*, like the platform's unequal distribution of profit and attention itself. Elites *do* often make the environment worse and block solutions, but to blame the problem of elite capture entirely on their moral successes and failures is to confuse effect for cause. The true problem lies in the system itself, the built environment and rules of interaction that produced the elites in the first place.

In games, there are clear boundaries of power between the designers and the players. The designers experience a wide scope of choice, while the choices they make become fixed features of the game for players. Gamers enter an environment and experience the rules of interaction and basic incentives laid out for them by the designers, without themselves having a say in any of these.

This environment is not so different from the real world as it might seem. As Carter G. Woodson realized, many of our decisions are shaped by decisions that someone with more power made before us. The whole social structure affects how institutional systems, like schools, function. In turn, those institutional systems exert power over the interactions that take place within them—conversations, lectures, relationships.

A game environment responds to most players in similar ways: they encounter the same rules, costs, and incentives. The social environment responds differently to different people, as David Lewis's conversation between master and slave reminds us. The paper in which Lewis invokes this conversation, called "Scorekeeping in a Language Game," concerns itself with the way background rules combine with our previous decisions to tell us what action makes sense for us to take at a specific juncture. Lewis uses baseball as an example to show how clear this is in a game context: whether the batter gets to walk to first base has to do with both the rules of the sport (including about how many balls any pitcher can throw before a batter walks) and how things have gone up until now (how many balls this pitcher has thrown on this particular at-bat).[30] But his earlier example of the master inventing rules for the slave on the fly more accurately describes many social interactions. After all, life is not nearly as fair as baseball.

As we saw in chapter 1, sufficiently powerful people and institutions are able to change, reconstruct, and ignore the rules of the game at will. While this works in different ways in different kinds of interactions and different parts of society, let's start where most of us hope to start our day: in a home. Under capitalism, an environment in which housing is commodified, whether someone has as an actionable choice to be housed or not depends greatly on the rules and rule-like actions of a small group of elites: individual landlords, corporate landlords, the police, and the data agencies that traffic information between these groups.[31] Elites have captured the means of maintaining shelter, so they set the rules by which the rest of us succeed or fail to win shelter.

What about the rest of your day? If you engage in any kind of economic activity whatsoever, then you are involved in some way with productive processes. And so, we encounter a familiar story of elite capture that ain't broke: the capitalists have captured the means of production. This is a familiar idea, but it is worth noting how, in doing so, they've also effectively captured huge swaths of human experience.

The social control held by capitalists in the production process claims as much of a worker's life and experience as employers can manage. Employers, not state governments, serve as the functional arbiters of workers' rights to freedoms of association and speech during the majority of their waking hours.[32] Sociologist Arlie Hochschild's much-belabored concept of "emotional labor" was originally a comment on the control bosses assert over the emotional expression of workers.[33] And, of course, elites structure workers' own access to the products that they spend so much time producing under their rules; working in health care doesn't guarantee you can afford your own.

Formal political structures are also famously plagued by elite capture. In a dismayingly literal fashion, laws are increasingly made by the powerful: in the United States, groups representing the interests of multibillion-dollar corporations, such as the American Legislative Exchange Council, write legislation that protects their interests, including bills that have criminalized protest against oil and gas infrastructure under the guise of "national security."[34]

Government regulators and courts, supposedly empowered to reign in the excesses of capitalists, often end up integrated into their profit-making plans instead—a process economists have helpfully termed "regulatory capture."[35]

Regulatory capture has dire consequences. In Nigeria, for instance, the relative power of regulation versus profit is so low that oil companies have either evaded regulatory fines or simply priced them into their business plans. A high-profile struggle of Ogoni people in 1993 to hold Shell accountable brought international attention to the ecological crisis in the Niger Delta caused by Shell's practices.[36] Despite the attention, Shell's behavior remained unchanged; in fact, researchers Enegide Chinedu and Chukwuma Kelechukwu Chukwuemeka found that oil spill incidents actually *increased* in the years after the controversy.[37]

Media (a field dominated by conglomerates in which advertising, public relations, and branding mingle with civic, social, artistic, and educational functions) are organized around attention and engagement. While "in the final analysis" these are often convertible into capital, many individuals feel that media creates a haven where we can escape some of the constraints that define our work lives and political experiences.[38] But, as with the material economy, those atop the attention economy exert the most influence over how the critical resources of attention and engagement are distributed.

Influential elites' (including social media "influencers") decisions about where to invest time or capital have outsize social effects that show up as fixed features of others' interactions. Their posts get engagement and attention, structuring which topics are trending, who Twitter's "main character" is for the day, and thus which topics are on the conversational agenda. When the rest of us make choices about what to watch or read or respond to, we're mostly making choices in an environment shaped by elites.

Does all of this sound familiar? Indeed it should after chapter 2. The genius of Carter G. Woodson was to see and articulate this pattern of elite capture in a history that began long before Twitter. Woodson put it plainly: "The so-called modern education, with all its defects, however, does others so much more good than it does the Negro, because it has been worked out in conformity to the needs of those who have enslaved and oppressed weaker peoples."[39] Woodson was analyzing how the rules of social interaction set by those in the "master" role in society affected the basic architecture of education, including the common ground of conversations held in classrooms.

It's bigger than conversation. Whole territories of social life have been captured by those at the top. This capture is built into the rules of engagement that result from colonial ownership. Capital accumulation is highly game-like in the clarity of its incentive structure, and its elite players have for several centuries been transforming the world so that more and more aspects of it become playable by the rules of capitalism. Most people end up playing along perforce, because the world as we find it at the level of individual interactions is an environment stocked with choices, penalties, and potential rewards that make sense in capitalist terms.

Whether it is a human manager or an Uber driver-rating algorithm telling the worker they should smile at the customer, the smile becomes an action that now makes sense for them to take, because playing along is the safest strategy for obtaining her objective—a paycheck.

Whether an oil-industry regulator accepts a bribe to look the other way or assiduously builds a fine and fee structure they know is bound to fail, they too are playing along.

Whether a student omits their own history from their paper because they believe the professor who said that Black people have no important history, or because they simply observe that the successful students always pick topics from white history, or because they can't find any books on Black history, they too are playing for the short-term win for themselves, following rules set down by someone else.

The game objective may be viscerally and irreducibly personal for each player—self-esteem, security, life itself—but the rules and the context that determine which actions make sense have been created by others who benefit from the outcome of those rigged systems.

The so-called common ground has been captured in the same way that oil regulatory infrastructures have. It is, after all, just "public information": things we treat as true together.

We use public information to do things—to communicate, yes, but also to do everything else that we do together.[40] As philosophers Kristie Dotson and Saray Ayala explain, it's a structure not so much of *beliefs*, but of "common epistemic resources" and "affordances": stuff built into the social environment that we can use to act together.[41] We act as if the information in the common ground is true, in the main, for much the same reason that we walk on sidewalks—it's easiest, and that's what it's there for.

Understood this way, common ground is just the informational aspect of the social environment that we build and rebuild with words and deeds. And when we successfully challenge the common ground, we are changing the social environment itself.[42]

3

Being in the Room

"In accepting to be led like sheep, European workers were perpetuating their own enslavement to the capitalists. . . . They failed to exercise any independent judgment on the great issues of war and peace, and therefore ended up by slaughtering not only colonial peoples but also themselves."
—Walter Rodney, *How Europe Underdeveloped Africa*[1]

"Without any doubt, underestimation of the cultural values of African peoples, based upon racist feelings and upon the intention of perpetuating foreign exploitation of Africans, has done much harm to Africa. But in the face of the vital need for progress, the following attitudes or behaviors will be no less harmful to Africa; indiscriminate compliments; systematic exaltation of virtues without condemning faults; blind acceptance of the values of the culture, without considering what presently or potentially regressive elements it contains; confusion between what is the expression of an objective and material

61

historical reality and what appears to be a creation of the
mind or the product of a peculiar temperament."
          —Amílcar Cabral, *Return to the Source*[2]

The last chapter may have been frustrating: all this talk about social structure, but what about our choices? Doesn't it matter how I decide to play the games life presents me? Aren't I free to respect the people around me, even if society says I should not—and aren't I to blame for my failures to do so, even if society encouraged those failures? How can elites have captured *everything*? And if they have, what's left? How can we possibly win in a world so thoroughly rigged and bought?

Yes, some forms of resistance to a rigged game are dead ends. They are anticipated by the designers, or pushback against the machinery leads only to marginal improvement, or resistance makes it worse.

We *can* do more than resist. We can do better. But before we can have a meaningful discussions about such tactics, it's really crucial to pay attention to what room the discussion is happening in.

What about right now? How did you and I get to be here, interacting across this page?

I could, after all, like many other people in the world, have simply read and thought about all of these issues on my own. I could even have spoken to my friends and colleagues about them. But that would not give me the power to speak to *you*.

According to the rules of racial capitalism, very few of the thousands or millions of people in the world who have some kind of insight into elite capture have the ability to enter a room where you, my reader, are available and open to listen to their thoughts. Maybe this book and the thoughts it contains are in the room with you only because of those rules. But maybe it's here with you in spite of them. Maybe the rules don't constrain us quite as much as I've suggested.

Activist and revolutionary Lilica Boal understood the difference between the rules that tell us who we are supposed to be and the actual choices we have when we act. After all, she was the sort of person who occasionally went off script, and who went into rooms she was not supposed to be in.

In June of 1961, the young Cape Verdean student was in a room she definitely was not supposed to be in: a Spanish prison.

Lilica should have known better. She was born in 1934 in the city of Tarrafal on the Cape Verdean island of Santiago, two years before the Portuguese Empire had built the Colónia Penal no Tarrafal (penal colony in Tarrafal), which housed antifascist dissidents to Portugal's dictatorial regime. The Boals were relatively well off for Cape Verdeans, especially for Black Cape Verdeans: in addition to owning property, her parents were merchants, and the penal colony was one of their customers.

Such middle-class status was not particularly easy to reach. For centuries, Portuguese colonial officials had conspired with plantation owners to prevent the islander Cape Verdeans from owning any nautical vessels, thus excluding the population from the food security and economic opportunities of the archipelago's considerable marine resources. This management was intimately tied to the empire's centuries-long use of the islands as a stopover point in the transatlantic slave trade, but also its persistent use of these islands as a containment area for exiled criminals, political deportees, and mutinous soldiers. For the Portuguese Empire, Cape Verde was, itself, a gulag.[3]

Lilica remembers watching trucks full of prisoners arrive to the prison, with panes installed to prevent anyone on the outside from seeing who was imprisoned inside of them. No one spoke of it, but everyone noticed: a constant warning about the price of defying the empire.[4]

Another linked episode from Lilica's childhood loomed large in her memory: the devastating famines of the 1940s, which claimed over forty-five thousand lives.[5] They were the latest in a succession of famines, which had been constant in Cape Verde over the centuries. These periods of extreme food scarcity were often blamed on droughts, but the real story was more complex, with wholly man-made elements. Low food production on the land was the result of soil depletion and erosion, which had been caused by centuries of unsustainable farming and herding practices on the island's plantations.[6] In addition to their outright subjugation, the vulnerability of Cape Verdeans to the problems on the farms was wildly exacerbated by the colonial prohibition on owning ships, which could have been used to supplement crops with seafood.[7]

For centuries, that man-made vulnerability to famine wrapped itself tightly around the island's racial hierarchy. At the top of the hierarchy were the few peninsular-born "super white" *brancos* (typically the governor, chief military officers, and top clergy). Just below them were the *brancos da terra*, or island-born whites, led by the old white *morgado* families who had been granted estates by the Portuguese crown. These landed proprietors were less than 5 percent of the population of the islands but owned and controlled virtually all of its arable land. Below these were mixed-race *pardos*, who were sometimes enslaved but often free, and were permitted some branco privileges, including European dress. At the bottom were the Black *pretos*. Enslaved pretos were often forced to work six days a week, leaving only one for the production of their own food; free pretos were forced into sharecropping arrangements that were not altogether dissimilar from outright slavery. Even after the abolition of slavery in 1864, which upended one crucial legal basis for this social structure, death from famine continued to correlate with the social status built by this hierarchy: brancos and pardos were likelier to own fruit trees and gardens, or valuables that they could sell for food when crisis struck—and, every few decades, it did.[8]

If they had been provided food aid from abroad, Cape Verdeans could possibly have survived even both of these problems, but by the 1940s the ruling Portuguese Empire had entered into what historian Alexander Keese calls "a dynamic of maximum exploitation of colonial populations." Their approach, which coupled indifference to colonial suffering with a lack of investment in basic infrastructure or administrative capacity, all but ensured that there would be plenty of suffering to go around.[9] Lilica recalls one occasion in which the Portuguese colonial administration responded to a plea for help from the governor of Cape Verde. They promptly sent money to the islands—to expand Tarrafal's cemetery.[10]

Lilica remembers much more: the bodies in the streets of those who had starved to death, the pots of food her family made to feed those around them. But she also remembers the remove she and the families of the prison guards felt from the struggle that surrounded them.[11] This changed when her family got a visit from a white Portuguese family.

Luís Alves de Carvalho and Dona Herculana were as out of place in Tarrafal as Lilica Boal would eventually be in Lisbon. The family was from Porto, a major city in Portugal, where Luís worked as a stockbroker. The draw of the small city of Tarrafal was not business opportunity, but the prison: it housed their antifascist teenage son, Guilherme da Costa Carvalho.[12]

The city of Tarrafal had neither a hotel nor even a restaurant. But a mutual business partner had told Luis about Lilica's family, who accepted the couple into their home. The Portuguese couple used the opportunity to visit with their son and his antifascist comrades.

Some time after the couple returned to Portugal, Lilica got the rare opportunity to enroll in college in Lisbon. There, they became Lilica's second family. When Guilherme was transferred out of Tarrafal to a prison in Portugal, she would go to the prison in Peniche to visit him.[13]

Partially through these visits, Lilica began to meet more and more leftists in Portugal. In addition to the incarcerated antifascists she met and heard of via her visits with Guilherme, the Portuguese couple introduced her to members of the Portuguese Communist Party like Virgínia Moura and Maria Cal Brandão, and involved the families of political prisoners in family get-togethers.[14] Later on, Lilica met and married her husband, Manuel Boal, a medical student from Angola, and their first daughter Sara was born soon after.

Perhaps the most important of these meetings came in 1960, when Lilica moved to Lisbon to spend time with the Casa dos Estudantes do Império (CEI; house of students of the empire). There, students in Lisbon from Angola, Mozambique, São Tomé, and Guinea-Bissau—Portugal's African colonies—all met to discuss the situations in their various countries and decide what contribution they could make. They figured that whatever they were going to do, they weren't going to do it in Lisbon. So they resolved to smuggle themselves out of the country and back to their respective homelands—the "flight to the fight." This was a particularly difficult decision for Lilica and Manuel, whose daughter was only seventeen months old, but the couple decided to send Sara to Lilica's mother in Tarrafal and join the charge.

Lilica and Manuel packed what belongings they could fit into a ten-pound suitcase and took off with other students they knew from the CEI. They made it to the border with Spain, bribing their way onto a small smuggling boat, but were caught and spent two days in a Spanish prison. There, Portuguese police asked their Spanish counterparts to turn them over to Portuguese authorities, but the Conselho Ecumenico das Igrejas (ecumenical council of churches) pressured the Spanish authorities into letting them continue on toward France. The couple and their comrades eventually made it to Germany, where they met a plane sent by the prime minister of Ghana, Kwame Nkrumah, that ferried the students to that country.[15]

Lilica remembers being "well received" there, but also plenty of skepticism about the newly arrived "young bourgeois students." According to Lilica, even Nkrumah himself once asked the Cape Verdean political leader Amílcar Cabral: "Do you think that this group is going to participate in the struggle?" But they did. Lilica went on to play an important role in Cape Verde and Guinea-Bissau's revolutionary struggle against the Portuguese Empire and its subsequent nation-building project, helping both to plan military strategy and to develop their approaches to education and solidarity-based international relations.[16]

Deference Politics

The history of Cape Verde and Guinea-Bissau and the deep racial, gender, class, religious, and other divisions cleaving the peoples of those places apart from each other makes it hard to understand how there was revolutionary struggle there at all, much less a successful one. The rules of social interaction would seem to rule out any kind of workable solidarity. Indeed, if Lilica had stuck to the social script, it's hard to see how she would have ended up in something like the PAIGC at all, much less in so pivotal of a role.

But the point of the last chapter was not that we are powerless in the face of history and social structure. It was, rather, to clarify how much of the game has already been played by the time society hands us the controller. Nonetheless, we can and do retain meaningful power and responsibility, even inside the mechanics of a game that is so powerfully rigged.

One way of responding to this rigged game is to focus on where we're at already. History has built the rooms around us; we find ourselves in places, and with people, resources, and incentives, that we did not choose.

The first rules we learn to follow are the ones that apply to the room we are in. The powers that be have decided those rules, including where the resources are and who is granted access to them. As we saw in the previous chapter, they even set the rules for how the environment responds to our actions, and frequently the environment is hostile. But they don't actually control, directly, what our actions are. So there is an opportunity here, of a sort.

When it comes to our interpersonal interactions inside the rooms of our daily lives, we can act on the basis of rules that we actively agree to—the emperor's rules be damned. We may not be able to control how the room reacts to our speech, but we *can* speak. We can also choose not to speak, to invite someone else in the room to speak, or to follow their lead.

These are the kinds of opportunities seized on by deference politics, which considers it a step toward justice to modify interpersonal interactions in compliance with the perceived wishes of the marginalized. While the deference perspective isn't entirely off base, it is potentially limiting and misleading. In such a game, it is much trickier than we realize to avoid moves that intensify elite capture and other oppressive aspects of our social structure—even when we use strategies that correctly identify the distribution of power in the room we're in.

After all, some rooms have outsize power and influence: the White House Situation Room, the newsroom, the bargaining table, the conference room. Being in one of *these* rooms means that our words and actions affect institutions and broader social dynamics outside of it. To be in such a room is itself a kind of social advantage, often gained by way of some prior social advantage.

A prime example of deference politics is the call to "listen to the most affected" or "center the most marginalized," now ubiquitous in many academic and activist circles. These calls have never sat well with me. In my experience as an academic and organizer, when people have said they needed to "listen to the most affected," it wasn't usually because they intended to set up Skype calls to refugee camps or to collaborate with houseless people. Acting on this conception of "centering the most marginalized" would require a different approach entirely, in a world where 1.6 billion people live in inadequate housing (slum conditions) and 100 million are unhoused, a full third of the human population does not have reliable drinking water, and the intersections of food, energy, and water insecurity with the climate crisis have already displaced 8.5 million people in South Asia alone, while threatening to displace tens of millions more.[17] Such a stance would require, at a minimum, that one leave the room.

Instead, "centering the most marginalized" in my experience has usually meant handing conversational authority and attentional goods to whoever is already in the room and appears to fit a social category associated with some form of oppression—regardless of what they have or have not actually experienced, or what they do or do not actually know about the matter at hand. Even in rooms where stakes have been high—where potential researchers were discussing how to understand a social phenomenon, where activists were deciding what to target—the rules of deference have often meant that the conversation stayed in the room, while the people most affected by it stayed outside.

This particular politics of deference emerged out of a theoretical orientation called standpoint epistemology, which became popular in feminist circles in the 1970s and has continued to contribute to the thinking of many activists and academics since.[18] Standpoint epistemology comprises three seemingly innocuous ideas:

1) knowledge is socially situated,

2) marginalized people have some advantages in gaining some forms of knowledge, and

3) research programs (and other areas of human activity) ought to reflect these facts.

These ideas should go down easy. As Liam Kofi Bright argues, any serious empiricist philosophy would entail all three of these points.[19] Moreover, they are politically important: they point to the value of lived experience and the knowledge that comes from it. At face value, a commitment to these ideas should help us resist and contain elite capture. They should provide a basis for respecting knowledge that the institutions of the world otherwise want to discredit.

But the devil is in the details. The common approaches to putting these abstract ideas into practice emphasize deference to others in conversational contexts, in an effort to fix the distribution of attention: they ask that we pass the mic, believe marginalized people, and give offerings.

The motivation is admirable, and these actions themselves are often good ideas, as far as they go. But aside from involving attitudes and interpersonal dynamics, oppression—racism, ableism, xenophobia, patriarchy, and so forth—also have serious *material* consequences. These structures of injustice decide who has reliable access to basic interpersonal security, housing, health care, water, and energy. All of these consequences of bigotry, from the attitudinal to the material, have to be dealt with if we are to address oppression.

The politics of deference focuses on the consequences that are likeliest to show up in the rooms where elites do most of their interacting: classrooms, boardrooms, political parties. As a result, we seem to end up with far more, and more specific, practical advice about how to, say, allocate tasks at a committee meeting than how to keep people alive.

Deference as a default political orientation can work counter to marginalized groups' interests. We are surrounded by a discourse that locates attentional injustice in the selection of spokespeople and book lists taken to represent the marginalized, rather than focusing on the actions of the corporations and algorithms that much more powerfully distribute attention. This discourse ultimately participates in the weaponization of attention in the service of marginalization. It directs what little attentional power we can control at symbolic sites of power rather than at the root political issues that explain why everything is so fucked up.

A trip down memory lane provides a powerful example of both the opportunities and limitations of the deferential approach. In 2007, Barack Obama was on the campaign trail for the US presidency. Obama had just lost two of the first three primary contests to Hillary Clinton. He gave a speech to a small crowd in Greenwood, South Carolina, looking exhausted and disheartened. Suddenly, an attendee named Edith S. Childs called out words of encouragement: "Fired up, ready to go!" People around her repeated the chant, and the energy in the crowd crescendoed. After a newly energized Barack Obama crushed Clinton in the South Carolina primary, those five words became a slogan of the campaign that carried the young upstart into the White House.[20]

Two years later, President Barack Obama went back out on the speaking trail—this time to Minneapolis, Minnesota, in defense of his fight to expand access to health care. President Obama explained that he "always believed that change doesn't come from the top down; it comes from the bottom up. . . . It begins with you sharing your stories, fighting for something better."[21] But what does change coming from the "bottom up" mean, in this context? The president was remarkably explicit: "[I]t goes to show you how one voice can change a room. And if it changes a room, it can change a city. And if it can change a city, it can change a state. And if it can change a state, it can change a nation. If it change[s] the nation, it can change the world." In other words, the president held forth a model of change flowing through approved channels and hierarchies atop which, ultimately, he stood.

We tend to be on our guard for this kind of cynical use of "bottom up" thinking by elites when we deal with politicians and formal, electoral politics. But, as political theorist

Jo Freeman has argued, our own rooms are not free of this phenomenon.[22] According to Freeman, any group of people interacting with each other will structure itself in some way or other, whether consciously or unconsciously, leaving only the question of how that resulting structure distributes resources, responsibilities, attention, and power.

Elites from marginalized groups can benefit from deference in ways that are at least compatible with social progress, especially if we take the right actions afterward. But treating such elites' interests as necessarily or even presumptively aligned with the broader group's interests involves a political naivete we cannot afford. In this context, confusion about elite interests functions as a form of racial Reaganomics: a strategy reliant on fantasies about the exchange rate between the attention economy and the material economy.

We need to fix the social structure itself—the rooms we interact in, and the house they make up. Deference, as a strategy, bears at best a tenuous relationship to this goal.

The View from Inside the Room

To say what's wrong with the popular, deferential applications of standpoint epistemology, we need to understand what makes it popular. First, a cynical answer: deference to figures from oppressed communities is a performance that sanitizes, apologizes for, or simply distracts from the fact that the deferrer has enough "in the room" privilege for their "lifting up" of a perspective to be of consequence—to reflect well on *them*.

In her influential essay "The Tyranny of Structureless-ness," Freeman notes that "structurelessness" in the women's liberation movement did not resolve the problem of unequal and unfair distributions of power; instead, it provided a mask behind which informal networks of well-positioned elites could hide their outsize influence on the culture and activities of the group.[23]

Unlike structurelessness, deference politics doesn't mask its distributive consequences. Visible performance of a deferential act of "passing the mic" or "stepping back" in order to give attention or space to another person does tend to redistribute short-term attention, as promised. But deference politics can still mask essential power relations, especially when we consider the performance in the context of the people who aren't in the room at all. For instance, one white person giving the mic to the specific person of color in the room can obscure both the overall power dynamics of the room and the whole room's relationship to the broader category of "people of color" that a particular comrade is taken to represent.

It would be reasonable to assume that most of those who practice standpoint epistemology deferentially do so for the right reasons, and that they trust the people they share the room with to help them find the proper practical expression of their joint moral commitments. Indeed, we don't need to attribute bad faith to all or even most of those who practice deferential politics to explain the phenomenon.

Bad roommates aren't the problem, for the same reason that being a good roommate isn't the solution: the problem is that we are still trapped in the room. If we want better politics, we have to challenge how those rooms are put together, the security system that controls access to them, and the rules that dictate what happens in them.

For illustration, we can return to the question of how you came to read this book—how it is that you and I are interacting through this text, right now. To do so, we have to consider the layers of history, politics, and geography that made its writing possible.

Many aspects of our social system serve as filtering mechanisms, determining which interactions happen and between whom, and thus, what social patterns people are in a position to observe. For the majority of the twentieth century, the US immigration quota system made legal immigration with a path to citizenship available almost exclusively to Europeans (earning Adolf Hitler's regard as the world "leader in developing explicitly racist policies of nationality and immigration," in the words of legal scholar James Q. Whitman).[24]

But the 1965 Immigration and Nationality Act opened up immigration possibilities to more people, with a preference for "skilled labor." My family migrated from Nigeria to the United States under these auspices, becoming part of the Nigerian American community that makes up one of the country's most successful immigrant populations. What no one mentions, of course, is that the 112,000 or so Nigerian Americans with advanced degrees are utterly dwarfed by the 82 million Nigerians who live on less than a dollar a day.

The selectivity of US immigration law helps explain the rates of educational attainment in the Nigerian diasporic community that raised me, which in turn helps explain the wealth, class advantages, and cultural expectations that fueled my own educational development.[25]

The class advantages I grew up with help explain which rooms I was educated and socialized in during elementary and middle school, which in turn help explain my entry into the exclusive Advanced Placement and honors classes in high school, while others from more disadvantaged backgrounds were routed through remedial courses. This in turn helps explain my access to higher education, which involved admission to schools from which others were rejected, and so on.

Indeed, the education system is a ready and uncommonly explicit example of selection processes. This is the trajectory that explains why *my* thoughts on elite capture were originally accepted and published as an article in *The Philosopher*,[26] and why I have the resources now to write a whole book that even nonphilosophers might read. It's a case in point of what sociological researchers call "cumulative advantage" or the "Matthew effect": the people who were successful yesterday are likeliest to get today's rewards, which makes them yet more likely to get tomorrow's as well.[27]

With these selections in view, it is easy to see how this deferential form of standpoint epistemology contributes to elite capture at scale. The higher the form of education, the narrower the social experience. Some students are pipelined to PhDs, while others are pipelined to prisons—and the very oppressive structures we aim to challenge largely explain who goes where. Deferential ways of dealing with identity can easily inherit the distortions caused by these selection processes.

But it's equally easy to see locally—in *this* room, in *this* social space, in *this* conversation—why deference seems to make sense. It may be an improvement on the epistemic procedure that preceded it. The Black person in the elite room may well be better positioned than non-Black people in this space to think about policing and incarceration. So, if we have to listen to one person, perhaps it's better that it be a Black person, even an affluent and privileged Black person, than the affluent and privileged white person who would otherwise have dominated the discussion. Put another way, deference can often seem like the best we can do in the face of what we take to be the fixed facts about the room and its purpose, and who's in it.

But these are the last facts we should want to hold fixed. And if our aim is simply to do better than the epistemic norms that we've inherited from a history of explicit global apartheid, that is an awfully low bar to set.

The facts that explain *who* ends up in *what* room shape our world much more powerfully than the squabbles for comparative prestige between people who have already made it inside. And when the conversation is about social justice, the social mechanisms that determine who gets into the room are often exactly what needs to change—for example, the fact that incarcerated people cannot participate in academic discussions about freedom is intimately related to the fact that they are physically locked in cages.

Still, deference does have attractive qualities. After all, the people in powerful rooms, to whom others defer, may be "elites" relative to the larger group they represent, but disadvantaged relative to the other people in the rooms with them.

Our sense of ourselves—and the patterns of deference we tend to fit to our standpoint epistemological commitments—often foregrounds the ways in which we are marginalized, rather than the ways we are not. A privileged person in an absolute sense (a person belonging to, say, the half of the world that has secure access to "basic needs") may nevertheless experience themselves consistently on the low end of the power dynamics of their immediate social world. The rooms we are in, which is to say the social dynamics we actually experience, play a central part in developing and refining our political subjectivity and our sense of ourselves.

Deference responds to real, morally weighty experiences of being put down, ignored, sidelined, silenced. The fact that others have graver problems does not legitimate bigotry toward the relatively advantaged.

People are—and ought to be—vying for respect, dignity, and some measure of recognition alongside policy reforms and material redistribution. We all deserve these attentional goods, which are often denied, even to the "elites" of marginalized and stigmatized groups. Moreover, distributions of respect and care can be won and lost collectively; there is *some* connection between the inside of the room and the outside. The deference interpretation of standpoint epistemology thus has an important non-epistemic appeal to such elites: it intervenes directly in morally consequential practices of giving attention and respect.

This focus on one's own relative marginalization is especially easy to cultivate when exposure to people below us in the relevant hierarchies is controlled or prevented, which is, after all, a great deal of what rooms do. This foregrounding of the personal happens for a reason that is entirely compatible with the ethos of "standpoint epistemology" and valuing lived experience. Our personal emphasis on the ways we are marginalized often matches the world *as we have experienced it*. And such a focus may be in some ways convenient for the practitioners of deference epistemology. Nonetheless, I still think that the cynical view does them too little credit. Many who practice deference epistemology are simply doing the best they can.

However, this same phenomenon also illustrates how the strength of standpoint epistemology, its recognition of the importance of perspective, becomes its weakness when flattened into deference politics. From a structural perspective, the rooms we *don't* enter, the experiences we *don't* have (and the reasons we are able to avoid them) might have more to teach us about the world and our place in it than anything said inside. If so, the deferential approach to standpoint epistemology actually *prevents* "centering" or even hearing from the most marginalized, since it focuses us on the interactions inside the rooms we occupy, rather than calling us to account for the interactions we needn't and typically don't have.

For those who are deferred to, the performance of deference can supercharge group-undermining norms.

In her book *Conflict Is Not Abuse*, activist writer and scholar Sarah Schulman makes a provocative observation about the psychological effects of both trauma and felt superiority: while these often come about for different reasons and have very different moral statuses, they result in similar behavioral patterns. Chief among these are misrepresenting the stakes of conflict (often by overstating harm) and representing others' independence as a hostile threat (for example, calling out failures to "center" the right topics or people). These behaviors, whatever their causal history, have corrosive effects, especially when a community's norms magnify or multiply rather than constrain or metabolize them.

For those who defer, the habit can supercharge moral cowardice, as the norms of deference provide social cover for the abdication of responsibility. It displaces onto individual heroes, a hero class, or a mythicized past the work that is ours to do in the present. Their perspective may be clearer on this or that specific matter, but their overall point of view isn't any less particular or constrained by history than ours. More importantly, deference places the accountability that is all of ours to bear onto select people—and, more often than not, a sanitized and thoroughly fictional caricature of them.

Deference to collectives or their culture has many of the same risks as deference to marginalized individual. PAIGC militant Amílcar Cabral affirmed the need to respond to centuries of anti-Black racism and the widespread assumptions about the inferiority of African history and culture. He, of course, denied that anything like a single African culture existed. But even if it did, reference to it would not answer questions about how we ought to behave and organize ourselves politically, since "all culture is composed of essential and secondary elements, of strengths and weaknesses, of virtues and failings, of positive and negative aspects, of factors of progress and factors of stagnation or regression." He went as far as to insist that "blind acceptance of the values of the culture, without considering what presently or potentially regressive elements it contains" would be "no less harmful to Africa" than racist underestimation of African culture had been.[28]

The same tactics of deference that insulate us from criticism and disagreement insulate us from connection and transformation. They prevent us from engaging empathetically and authentically with the struggles of other people—a prerequisite of coalitional politics.

Moreover, as identities become more and more fine grained and disagreements sharper, we come to realize that "coalitional politics" (understood as struggle across difference) is, simply, politics. Thus, the deferential orientation, like that fragmentation of political collectivity it enables, is ultimately anti-political.

To opt for deference, rather than interdependence, may soothe short-term psychological wounds. But it does so at a steep cost: it may undermine the goals that motivated the project—and it entrenches a politics that does not serve those fighting for freedom over privilege, for collective liberation over mere parochial advantage.

Better Blueprints

Deference politics is right about the *what*: it does in fact matter that we pay attention to lived experiences, and it is politically important that we pay attention to difference. But it is wrong about the *how*, because the more we focus on changing our norms of interactions to ones that locally and cosmetically elevate the voices and perspectives *in* the room, the harder it becomes to change the world *outside* of the room.

As philosopher C. Thi Nguyen reminded us in the last chapter, the power of the system is that of the game designer. It builds our social, economic, cultural, and even attentional environment in ways that get us to follow its game plan.

In the speech I quoted at the beginning of this chapter, Amílcar Cabral explains another important aspect of this systemic control: "[I]mperialist domination . . . for its own security, requires cultural oppression and the attempt at direct or indirect liquidation of the essential elements of the culture of the dominated people." Culture, for Cabral, is our collective ability to design and organize our own lives, and be the engines of our own history—an ability that conflicts directly with the aims of imperialists to be the ones doing the designing and controlling. This is why, "whatever may be the material aspects of this domination," imperialist domination can survive "only by the permanent, organized repression of the cultural life of the people concerned."[29]

This, above all, illustrates the key problem with deference: it focuses the very capacity that we have to reconstruct the whole house to the specific rooms that have already been built for us. It advertises itself as deferring to marginalized voices and perspectives, but in conceding so much creative space to the blueprint of society, it is perhaps better understood as deference to the built structure of society.

I am arguing here for another approach—one that concedes that we have to start with the interactions that we have most control over, but that keeps in view the point of changing how those interactions go: to rebuild the whole of society, not just our interactions. Rooting ourselves here thus gives us a *constructive* politics.

A constructive politics pursues specific goals or end results, rather than aiming to avoid "complicity" in injustices that we assume will mostly persist anyway. If it's "epistemology" or knowledge practices we're concerned about, then a constructive politics focuses on institutions and practices of information gathering that are strategically useful for challenging social injustices themselves, not just the symptoms manifest in the room we happen to be in today.

In general, a constructive politics is one that engages directly in the task of redistributing social resources and powe,r rather than pursuing intermediary goals cashed out in symbols.

This is a demanding approach. It asks that we swim upstream, that we be accountable and responsive to people who aren't yet in the room, and that we build the kinds of rooms in which we can sit together, rather than merely seek to navigate more gracefully the rooms history has built for us.

The task of rebuilding the world is demanding—and it's constructive politics, not deferential politics, that brings these demands together.

4

Building a New House

"Resistance is the following: to destroy something, in order to build something else. That's what resistance is. What do we want to destroy on our land? The colonial domination of the Portuguese soldiers. Just that by itself? No—at the same time, we don't want any other time of colonial domination on our land, or any other kind of foreign domination. We want our people to determine their own destiny, through their children, in Guinea and Cape Verde. This is our primary objective."
—Amílcar Cabral, *Análise de Alguns Tipos de Resistência*[1]

Paulo Freire had a very hungry childhood.

Still, it could have been worse. Freire was born in Recife, Brazil, in 1921—a place he would later call "the center of one of the most extreme situations of poverty and underdevelopment in the Third World."[2] The Freires were a temporarily precarized middle-class family whose normal economic security was upset by the exceptional circumstances of the Great

Depression.[3] As such, Paulo and his siblings were "connective kids," socially linked with both the well-off and the poor.

But the hunger that bound him by common experience to the children from the "poor outskirts of town" did not do so without qualification: he and his siblings were still "people from another world who happened to fall accidentally into their world."[4] While hunger arrived to his family "unannounced and unauthorized, making itself at home without an end in sight," it arrived to a living room with a piano and a household led by a man who wore a necktie to work—markers of class status that the Freires clung to for dear life.

Perhaps as a result, hunger came and went from their family before it could have the consequences that it had for millions of the working-class Brazilians in the "other world" that the Freire kids chanced upon. For many of these childhood friends, legs, arms, and fingers had been rendered thin and brittle, eyes had retreated into sockets—signs of persistent malnutrition, the kind of hunger that brought a moving truck instead of a suitcase.

Even so, Paulo never forgot. During his six years of exile, having fled the Brazilian military dictatorship that took power via a US-backed coup in 1964, he documented these experiences in what would become his most influential book, *Pedagogy of the Oppressed*.[5] The book introduces key ideas, including his criticism of what he called the banking model of education, in which teachers view poor students as passive, empty receptacles to be filled with the information they, the teachers, possess.[6]

This model, and the unchanging roles of the conferring teacher and receptive student that it assumes, are obstacles to be overcome. In the education of children and adults alike, the banking model attempts to create "automatons" who neither think nor act for themselves—and to prevent *conscientização* (critical consciousness), the mutually humanizing relationship between those from "oppressed" and "oppressor" backgrounds that results from a mutually liberatory education.[7]

Conscientização aims at the opposite of elite capture. While both elite capture and conscientização bring elites and non-elites together, elite capture perpetuates and exploits the divide by conscripting non-elites into the service of elites' interests; conscientização, on the other hand, aims to pursue the kind of mutually liberatory political project that would eliminate the distinction between elites and non-elites entirely.

This liberatory approach to education, Paulo argued, would begin by acknowledging the knowledge students and teachers both bring into any situation. But it would end with the transformation of the social relations that relied on their "education" into life as cogs in someone else's machine in the first place—that is, society itself. So he got to work, starting in the spaces to which he had access and in which he had power: classrooms.

Rebuild the House: Lilica, Paulo, and the PAIGC

The story of our global political system—the big house in which we all occupy rooms—begins with the explorations and conquests of the Portuguese Empire. In the previous chapter, we saw how Lilica Boal made a daring escape from the school room she was in. The struggle she left to join was the one taking place against the Portuguese Empire.

Long before Christopher Columbus set sail under the Spanish flag in 1492—the same year that the year the Christian powers finally removed the last Muslim dynasty from the Iberian Peninsula (completing the so-called Reconquista)—Portugal had long been hard at work building the colonies and trade relationships that would produce the transatlantic slave trade and thereby the modern world economy.[8]

Portuguese explorers sailed the western coast of Africa for the majority of the fifteenth century, claiming exclusive rights for Portugal for its "lands of discoveries." Armed and enriched by imperial conquests in Asia, Africa, and the Americas, and the riches they provided in precious metals and trafficked human beings, Portugal became the first modern superpower and, for a time, the richest country in Europe.[9]

Two of these "discoveries" were what would become today's countries of Guinea-Bissau and Cape Verde. Explorers landed in Guinea-Bissau in 1446 and the nearby archipelago of Cape Verde in 1456. The former was then the center of the Mandinka kingdom of Kaabu, whose *mansas* (rulers) exercised influence over broad swaths of western Africa with power gained from control over a hub of trans-Saharan trades of gold, ivory, and slaves.[10]

The captives from Kaabu's wars on the continent began to be sold into a new network of human trafficking that would far eclipse the network on the continent in size, scale, and depth of exploitation: the transatlantic slave trade, which funneled enslaved people and their labor into European colonial conquests.[11]

Most of these colonial territories, particularly in the initial centuries, were in the Americas. But Cape Verde was an exception. The chain of islands off Africa's western coast, un-inhabited and well suited as a stopover point in the emerging transoceanic trade, was then populated by Portuguese settlers and enslaved Africans. Cape Verde was also used as a staging point in the conquest of much of western Africa, including Guinea-Bissau, and Cape Verdeans were often afforded a middle managerial role in the both the slave trade and the colonial management of Guinea-Bissau.

By the time Lilica was born, well into the 1900s, European countries had used the wealth and power built up via the slave trade and their other global colonial efforts to establish formal colonial dominion over the vast majority of the African continent, including Cape Verde and Guinea-Bissau (then "Portuguese Guinea"). The Portuguese had long controlled their colonies with the callous indifference to suffering that was characteristic of the slave trade that the islands themselves enabled.

In response to one of the many droughts that plagued Cape Verde in the centuries leading up to its independence movement, colonial officials in London told a protesting Cape Verdean lawyer that "the government is not culpable that in Cabo Verde there have not been regular rains."[12] In all likelihood, Lilica's childhood was not so dissimilar from that of her parents or grandparents.

Portuguese militaries put down resistance to their rule with brutal military "pacification campaigns" to terrorize those who the famines and precarity did not silence.[13] This militarist posture was only intensified by the disintegration of the Portuguese democratic republic in 1926, which was replaced by a fascist regime installed under corporatist autocrat António Salazar called Estado Novo—the new state.[14]

In 1960, an organization rose to challenge the Estado Novo in Cape Verde and nearby Guinea-Bissau: the African Party for the Independence of Guinea and Cape Verde (PAIGC). The party spent three years negotiating with the Portuguese government, employing a strategy that focused on demonstrations and workers' strikes. The PAIGC's nonviolence was met with brutality, culminating in the massacre of fifty peacefully striking dockworkers at the port of Pidjiguiti.[15] After the massacre, the group began an armed guerrilla campaign of resistance to the Portuguese. This is the fight Lilica left school to join, and it culminated in the independence of both nations in 1973 and 1974.[16]

A number of factors contributed to the success of the PAIGC's multifaceted campaign, including the wave of African and Asian independence movements of the post–World War II decades (spearheaded by Ghana's independence in 1957) and the networks of mutual aid and solidarity that linked many of them, and particularly the African countries fighting against Portuguese domination (including Angola and Mozambique).

Historian Sónia Vaz Borges directs our attention toward an often-neglected aspect of their revolutionary activity: the PAIGC's militant education and consciousness raising practices.[17] Cape Verde and Guinea-Bissau inherited a colonial education system that was designed to produce and educate an elite class of "assimilated Africans" to comanage the colonial project and convert unassimilated "indigenous" Africans into a viable workforce.[18] By contrast, the militants of the PAIGC developed a program of education designed to counteract the ills of the Portuguese colonial education system and support self-determination and resistance to colonial rule.

The PAIGC's military struggle thus included a comprehensive battle on the "education front," which Bissau-Guinean militant Agnelo Regala said was considered "as important" as other fronts "because it is not worth . . . freeing the land if we are not ready to assume the responsibility of independence."[19] Basic literacy and political education were considered training for every aspect of the struggle.[20]

Through interviews with living PAIGC militants and archival research, Vaz Borges finds that they overcame a number of considerable practical hurdles. The PAIGC created and distributed a newspaper, even though low literacy rates among adults posed a challenge to its effectiveness. At the same time, schooling for children competed with their labor on the family farms and thus threatened the livelihood and survival of families who sustained themselves with subsistence farming. Partially as a result, the PAIGC's insistence on girls' inclusion in schools met with resistance in some parts of the countries. Security concerns and resource constraints, both exacerbated by the simultaneous armed struggle against the Portuguese military, always loomed large. Moreover, the PAIGC's secular education system threatened to interrupt a balance of power that had been carefully negotiated between the Portuguese, the Christian education system, and two other systems favored by the countries' Muslim and Animist communities.[21]

The PAIGC rose to meet these challenges through its cultivation of careful, strategic relationships, including with the newly formed Organization of African Unity, whose Liberation Committee served as a conduit for foreign material and military assistance to many of the anti-colonial movements on the continent, including from the Soviet Union and post-revolutionary China, which both donated substantial weapons and military training. Cuba, not content merely to contribute material assistance in the form of food and military uniforms, deployed troops—a step no other country took during the conflict.[22]

Ahmed Sékou Touré, president of the newly independent country of Guinea (neighboring Guinea-Bissau), donated a facility for a pilot boarding school. The party built the Escola Piloto with resources gained from the Red Cross and a high-ranking United Nations official (reputedly a "friend" to the liberation struggle). Lilica Boal was named the school's director.

Against this coalition was a parallel one lined up behind the Portuguese fascist state. Portugal, a NATO member, bombed Guinea-Bissau with the support of dozens of transport and bomber aircraft provided by Great Britain, France, Germany, the United States, and the American Lockheed corporation (now Lockheed Martin).[23]

The pilot school took in the children of PAIGC militants and the war orphans created by Portuguese bombs and infantry. There, Lilica and her comrades taught students, with considerable support from elsewhere in the world: they used materials printed in Sweden and funded partly by the Swedish Social Democratic Party, fed the children with provisions donated from Cuba (whose government also dispatched doctors to provide them health care), and maintained a laboratory for the students with resources from abroad.[24]

But, Vaz Borges explains, the PAIGC didn't stop at schools for children. They supplemented their adult and youth newspapers with collective reading and discussion circles, which especially facilitated adult education. To make children's education work, the party negotiated with village elders, working out a system in which children attended both PAIGC schools and religious schools, and integrated religious symbolism into party traditions.[25] They sent a contingent of women to the Soviet Union to receive education in nursing. After they returned, more girls enrolled. To facilitate the participation of children in a country of subsistence farmers, the school sessions were designed around the agricultural calendar.[26]

The full involvement of women in the liberation struggle was an explicit goal of the organization and was reflected in its organizing practices and regulations. For instance, the party eventually required that each of the elected village councils that helped organize the liberated zones include at least two women in its membership of five.[27] According to researcher Stephanie Urdang, from the time the first PAIGC mobilizers went to the countryside to hold consciousness-raising discussions in 1959, the party took only a decade to go from holding meetings that included just a handful of women to rough parity between men and women.[28] The armed wing of the party included a women's militia, which also produced many of the party's public health advisors.[29]

Cape Verde and Guinea-Bissau defeated the Portuguese Empire, winning national independence in 1973—an independence that was eventually recognized by the Portuguese government in 1975 after the previous year's revolution ousted the fascist Estado Novo regime.

The PAIGC went to work, transitioning from an armed struggle to one of a different kind: nation building. After seizing power in September 1973, the number of students in party programs more than doubled. But, having been focused on fighting the military, the party lacked the number of teachers needed for this new challenge. Nor did it have sufficient material resources to make new educational materials and quickly train cadres in the new educational method they had developed through the liberation struggle. As a result, Lilica Boal and her comrades felt their only option was to use existing colonial Portuguese educational materials and structures, but to "safely transform them."[30]

Paulo Freire and the Institute for Cultural Action (IDAC), of which he was a member and founder, were brought on to serve as advisors. This was in part because of the similarities in perspective between the framework for education the PAIGC had developed during the liberation struggle (aided by the pioneering contribution of the militants of the pilot school) and the theory Freire had elaborated before his exile from Brazil.[31]

Despite these efforts, there was no fairy-tale ending. The war with Portugal had destroyed much of Guinea-Bissau's infrastructure, cutting available arable land to less than a third of prewar levels—partially as a result of the Portuguese military's extensive bombing campaigns and herding of villagers who wouldn't (or couldn't) align with the PAIGC into small, dense farming plots that rapidly exhausted the soil.[32]

Economic crisis in Guinea-Bissau exacerbated social divisions: between the party and traditional leaders, between urban and rural parts of the countries, between different ethnic groups, and, perhaps most significantly, between Bissau-Guineans and Cape Verdeans. The Cape Verdeans, who were said to occupy a disproportionate number of leadership positions in the party, were often urban intellectuals whose participation had different stakes from the peasantry exposed to the worst of the war's violence and suffering, since nearly all of the early fighting of the war took place in Guinea-Bissau.[33] Moreover, the Cape Verdeans were likely deeply resented for the islands' long preferential treatment by the Portuguese Empire and middle managerial role in colonial domination.[34]

These tensions culminated in a 1980 coup that ousted the Cape Verdean wing of the party, which became the African Party for the Independence of Cape Verde (PAICV), remaining a major party in Cape Verdean politics to this day. Guinea-Bissau has been plagued by a pattern of coups and countercoups ever since, as different factions have fought for power in and around the party; in turn, power has become increasingly concentrated in the hands of party elites, including the ex-PAIGC militants.[35] Bissau-Guinean historian Julião Soares Sousa laments what he takes to be the products of the country's "painful recent history": the stigma brought by the fights for power and control, Guineans' lack of confidence in the political system and the party, the lack of effective action by the new elites in the face of the country's mounting problems, and, underlying all of the above, a deep-seated perversion of values.[36]

Making matters worse, increased policing of drug trafficking in Latin America made Guinea-Bissau a center of
the global illicit drug trade, particularly of cocaine. Just as
their location on Africa's western coast made Cape Verde and
Guinea-Bissau strategic locations for the transatlantic slave
trade, drug traffickers flocked to Guinea-Bissau as a stopover
point between Venezuela and Colombia, and the lucrative
European drug market. Global media christened Guinea-Bissau "Africa's first narco-state," estimating that as much as
a quarter of the world's cocaine was trafficked through the
small nation, though scholars tend to temper such claims.[37]
Recent trends, including an "all-time high" of global cocaine
consumption, have led some commentators to speculate that
drug traffickers may be trying to expand trafficking both in
and through Cape Verde in a similar fashion.[38]

Nevertheless, something meaningful was won, beyond
new flags. Even Guinea-Bissau, regarded by many as a "failed
state" (when not as a "narco-state"), has won some ground.[39]
Education is one such arena: using its newfound national
independence, Guinea-Bissau's literacy rate surged from its
pre-independence level of 2 percent, climbing as high as 60
percent among fifteen- to twenty-four-year-olds.[40]

In the decades since independence, Cape Verde increased
its national income tenfold, ascending from a status as one
of the poorest countries in the world to a "middle-income
country" and one of Africa's most stable economies.[41] The
PAIGC's emphasis on community power and decision making seems to have survived, avoiding the temptations toward
autocracy to which other revolutions succumbed, and some

foreign commentators have gone as far as to call it an "African exception" and "Africa's most democratic nation."[42]

These revolutionary struggles did not just liberate Cape Verde and Guinea-Bissau—they also liberated Portugal. Lilica Boal recalls the insistence of Amílcar Cabral, one of the PAIGC's leaders, that their struggle was against colonialism as a system, not against the people of Portugal.[43] The party followed through on this commitment in deed as well.[44] Carmen Pereira, a high ranking political commissar and among the most prominent members of the party, explained the party's position on identity politics to journalist Suzanne Lipinska in simple terms that we should take to heart: "There are white people who oppress us and there are ones who help us."[45] In a radio address in 1969 aptly titled "Message to the People of Portugal," Cabral made this plain to the whole world, explicitly positioning the PAIGC as on the side of the Portuguese people against the Estado Novo government.[46]

While this was undoubtedly clever wartime propaganda, it was more than that. The PAIGC showed leniency to Portuguese prisoners of war, often releasing them—attempting to go beyond words and communicate in deed the difference between themselves and the Portuguese army, which often summarily executed PAIGC militants who had the misfortune of falling into enemy hands.[47] Cabral, like many of his and Lilica's comrades from Portugal's African colonies, was educated in Lisbon—there, he had been a leading member of antifascist groups, taking risky political action against the Estado Novo regime with Black comrades like Agostinho

Neto of Angola and white comrades like Mário Soares (future leader of the Portuguese Socialist Party and also future president of post–Estado Novo Portugal).[48] Ethnic Studies scholar Reiland Rabaka describes Cabral's thinking as "global and historical theory," with political aims and aspirations to match: Cabral recognized imperialism as the structure of the whole planet, not just of conditions in Cape Verde and Guinea-Bissau, and he thus recognized that countering imperialism required changing everyone's political structure and not just that of his own people's.[49]

But it would also prove to be more than a mere symbolic stance of solidarity with his comrades. The colonial wars in Guinea-Bissau, as well as in Angola and Mozambique, were steadily eroding support for the Estado Novo regime among capitalist and clergy elites alike.[50] Four years after Cabral's address, left-wing military officers met in secret to challenge the Estado Novo regime; many of them met and plotted in Guinea-Bissau, the theater of the anti-colonial battles where the Portuguese military forces were most seriously contemplating defeat.[51] These officers eventually formed the Armed Forces Movement (MFA) that toppled the Estado Novo regime after it failed to meet the movement's core demands of the "three Ds": democracy, development, and decolonization.[52] Their largely bloodless (in Portugal, anyway) takeover is now known as the Carnation Revolution of 1974—so named because of the many images that circulated of ecstatic citizens handing soldiers carnations to celebrate the end of the fascist regime.[53] Though many underline the Carnation Revolution as a key turning point leading to decolonization, sociologist António Tomás points out that this idea is exactly backward: it was the revolutionary struggles of the PAIGC and their various comrades-in-arms that precipitated Portugal's partial decolonization, not the other way around.[54]

We've Got This

The PAIGC took on an important struggle against long odds, and their victories changed things for everyone. They could not erase or undo the barriers history had erected, but they could and did surpass many of them.

Chapters 2 and 3 painted a stark picture. Not only does social structure shape the environments in which we act with each other into worlds that serve elite interests, but it can subtly pervert our attempts to resist this elite domination. Some of the very actions we take to resist oppressive hierarchies end up serving them. Not exactly a hopeful turn.

But not all is lost. As we saw in the discussion of fable of the emperor's imaginary wardrobe, power structures affect even our most mundane interactions. But the conclusion of that story is equally consequential: a small child points and laughs at the emperor, failing to follow the rules or be intimidated. The spell of structural hierarchy is broken, and everyone can say aloud what they all were thinking: the emperor has no clothes!

There's a clear sense in which social structures organize our interactions: it builds the world in which they happen. This includes "affordances," usable aspects of the built social environment. If you want to make something easy to carry, give it a handle. If you want people to avoid having to walk on the road, pave a sidewalk and paint a crosswalk.

The world in which we act also includes incentives, the carrots and sticks that guide our behavior. In general, people are more likely to do things for which they're rewarded and less likely to do things for which they are punished.

There are limitations, of course. Social structures entail strong constraints that can render certain actions not just undesirable or unpopular, but literally impossible. One cannot "decolonize" the curriculum of a school that was not built in the first place. More darkly: a person cannot organize against your government if they have mysteriously fallen out of a helicopter or been imprisoned in a black site.

There are other strong and similarly effective forms of constraint: the terror inflicted on the loved ones of those thrown from helicopters, the physical presence of the surveilling overseer or manager. As Noam Chomsky put it in *Media Control:* "In what is nowadays called a totalitarian state, or a military state, it's easy. You just hold a bludgeon over their heads, and if they get out of line you smash them over the head."[55]

But these strongarm forms of restraint usually involve costly interventions. They require more attention and money, and invite more severe reprisals than elites tend to care to risk.

This is why most social structures rely on weaker enforcement mechanisms to police social life. They build affordances that herd people into the behavior that they would like, making it easy to do things that support the system and difficult to do things that do not. The upshot is that they maintain unbalanced and self-protective distributions of reward and punishment.

A classic way of doing this is to manipulate information through propaganda and disinformation. It's worth remembering that our information environment—our "systems of education," to use Carter G. Woodson's term—are less about strong-arm indoctrination of people and more about making system-preserving uses of information easy while rendering system-altering uses of information difficult.

Misinformation and propaganda often succeed at misleading, distracting, and misinforming. But they needn't. What's important politically is the result of such efforts in terms of what people do and don't do. There are reasons other than bad ideas, as we've already seen, that someone might compliment the emperor's robe or avoid making fun of him.

Some aspects of social policing are focused squarely on changing people's decisions without directly changing what they think. For instance, a wide range of activist groups, including the Debt Collective and the Movement for Black Lives, along with thinkers like Fantu Cheru and Jeffrey Williams, have long noticed the disciplinary function of student, medical, and credit card debt.[56] Cheru argues that external debts pressured postrevolutionary African governments into deals with the International Monetary Fund, while Williams shows how mounting student debt in the United States is itself a new "mode of pedagogy" that is driving students out of disruptive organizing and into docile compliance with the status quo.[57]

But there's also a clear sense in which all of this world building and policing *fails* to constrain us. Creatures like us have a special power. Despite all our social programming, we can just *do* things. We can, to some extent at will, ignore what social structures have told us to do. We can ignore the sidewalk and walk in the street; we can carry the bag with handles from its underside. We can do the thing that will be punished; we can ignore the potential reward, choose the smaller prize. Moreover, we can accept the rewards and the punishments without accepting the "lessons" they are meant to teach us about who and what is worthy.

It is this kind of action, off the beaten path, that the small child takes when they see the emperor. It is also what Carter G. Woodson did in response to white supremacy, what Lilica Boal and her PAIGC comrades did in the face of Portuguese colonialism, and what Paulo Freire did in response to the hierarchies of Brazilian racial capitalism and the geopolitics of the Cold War.

Immense structures and entrenched interests spend immense time, money, and effort convincing us either that we do not have this power or that we had better not use it. It is not hard to see why: it is the kind of power that can very quickly turn the talk of the town into the butt of its jokes.

This power is one of many that helps explain why our social systems are not fixed—even ones as complicated as our current global system of capitalism. As we already saw with the common ground, its structure is something we can and do change regularly. We can walk in the street, even when there are sidewalks; we can drive on the wrong side of the road; we can read sentences from right to left. As you can tell from these examples, we don't necessarily have much to gain from engaging in just any old deviation from the social script. But with some effort and thoughtfulness, this is a power we can wield more constructively: We can decide to share information the boss tells us is sacrosanct. We can walk in the street to block traffic for the protest. And we can invite people to do these things with us.

Our capacity to make the systems we live in more complex, even while embedded in a world that structures our actions, is itself part of the system's overall *self-organization*, as environmental scientist and systems theorist Donella Meadows explains. Meadows notes a role for education that is strikingly similar to the one Woodson envisaged nearly a century earlier: "[C]onditions that encourage self-organization often can be scary for individuals and threatening to power structures. As a consequence, education systems may restrict the creative powers of children instead of stimulating those powers."[58]

Human social systems are self-organizing. Indeed, something much like this thought is already embedded in the use of the term "organizing" to label work that challenges oppressive aspects of our society. Often when we organize, we try to build a smaller system of our own within the overall system we live in that is influential enough to change the whole system's behavior. This is a potential role for a mass movement, a workers' party, a set of direct actions. It's the sort of thing we can do in a room.

In both Cape Verde and Guinea-Bissau, the PAIGC ran into obstacles to achieving a deeper freedom, beyond having a flag and ministers. This included internal dynamics, social cleavages that they could manage but not erase. But they also included external problems beyond the immediate control of their interpersonal dynamics and institutional choices, including resource constraints and the global drug trade.

In our organizing, there are two basic ways we can respond to this unfortunate fact about political struggle. The first is to shift our aims and priorities to focus on that which we can easily reach, either by ignoring the external constraints or simply by taking on faith that getting the "internal" politics right is our best shot of changing the world at large. While there is a wisdom to focusing on what we have the best chance of controlling or managing, this approach is also deeply defeatist. That's why, in any sober analysis of our situation, most of the tools we have to affect to change the world are part of a second, "external" strategy: one that lies outside of any given room or set of interpersonal relationships.

Getting Out the Hammers

If we follow the constructive approach that I am advocating in these pages, we recognize that the way we treat each other in organizing spaces matters primarily in terms of how it relates us to the rest of the world. After all, most of the world—and thus most of the structures we are trying to change—are outside of the particular rooms in which we build alliances and refine our politics.

Whatever the PAIGC got wrong, they got this right: both the militant education of the liberation struggle and the postrevolutionary construction of an education system were part and parcel of the same effort: one to change not just the dynamics of the classroom, but those of a whole society. They aimed to literally redraw the map of the world and change its power relations, and they tried to build the kinds of rooms that would support that outcome.

The water-contamination crisis in Flint, Michigan, presents another, more recent example of both the possibilities and limitations of refining our politics in this way. Michigan's Department of Environmental Quality (MDEQ), a government body tasked with the support of "healthy communities," with a team of fifty trained scientists at its disposal, was complicit in covering up the scale and gravity of the public health crisis for months after the 2014 switch of the city's water source to the heavily polluted Flint River.

After the American Civil Liberties Union circulated a leaked internal memo from the federal Environmental Protection Agency that expressed concern about lead in Flint water, the MDEQ produced a doctored report, putting the overall measure of lead levels within federally mandated levels by failing to count two contaminated samples. The MDEQ, speaking from a position of expertise and political authority, defended the status quo in Flint, claiming that "Flint water is safe to drink," which Flint mayor Dayne Walling cited in his statement aiming to "dispel myths and promote the truth about the Flint River."[59]

The month after the ill-fated switch in Flint's water source, residents reported that their tap water was discolored and gave off an alarming odor. In that moment, what they needed was not for their oppression to be "celebrated," "centered," or narrated in the newest academic parlance. They didn't need outsiders to empathize over what it felt like to be poisoned. To be sure, deference politics could give people these things—and these things aren't unimportant. But they are secondary. What Flint residents really needed, above all, was to get the lead out of their water.

So they got to work. The first step was to develop epistemic authority. To achieve this, they built a new room, one that put Flint residents and activists in active collaboration with scientists who had the laboratories to run the relevant tests and prove MDEQ's report was fraudulent.

Flint residents' outcry about the poisonings helped recruit scientists to their cause. The new roommates ran a citizen science campaign, further raising the alarm about the water quality and distributing sampling kits to neighbors so that they could submit their water for testing. The alliance of residents and scientists won, and the poisoning of the children of Flint emerged as a national scandal.

This victory over the public narrative was only a first step, however. The second step—cleaning the water—required more than state acknowledgment; it entailed the apportionment of labor and resources to fix the water and address continuing health concerns.

What Flint residents received, initially, was a mix of platitudes and mockery from the ruling elite (including the US president, whose shared racial identity with many of the Flint residents apparently did not constrain). Now, however, it looks as though the activism of Flint residents and their expanding list of coalition partners has won additional and more meaningful victories. As of this writing, the ongoing campaign is pushing the project to replace dangerous water service lines to its final stage and has already forced the State of Michigan to pay a $600 million settlement to affected families.

This outcome is in no way a wholesale victory. Not only will attorney fees cut a substantial portion from the payouts, but the settlement cannot undo the damage that was caused to the residents.

Indeed, no epistemic orientation can by itself undo the various power asymmetries between the people and the imperial state system. But constructive politics, like that of Flint's residents *can* help make the game a little more competitive; deference epistemology, on the other hand, isn't even playing.

Building a New House

At the end of the day, there's only so much we can accomplish in the room—in our organization, on our block, in our academic department, in our party. Getting the dynamics of our movements, communities, friend groups, and social networks right is important, but there's also the crucial question of how that internal work relates to other struggles.

Racial capitalism is itself a global system, and the pace and direction of the climate crisis it has wrought will be set by our successes and failures at that same planetary scale.[60]

At bottom, the constructive approach responds to this problem in a very simple fashion. Whether on a small scale or in a large institution, our orienting political goal is to *build things*, whether institutions, norms, or other tools. As we've just seen, the residents of Flint built a citizen-science structure to challenge the MDEQ. This is not a one-off story, but a generalizable strategy: even public decision-making that involves technical concepts and research can be done in a meaningfully democratic and participatory fashion.[61]

Like standpoint epistemology, this simple ethos seems obvious and innocuous enough at this level of abstraction. But it has competitors. For instance, people and organizations could orient their politics oppositionally. Many forms of political identification consist in whole or in large part as lists of things that one opposes: one is "anti-capitalist," "anti-carceral," or "antiracist." Racism, capitalism, and mass incarceration are worth opposing. But the long view of human history confirms that even successful opposition to these would not guarantee a just future. Not one of these phenomena, at least in their modern forms, is even a millennium old. Especially in recent history, more often than not, one form of oppression has been replaced with another, different form that is similar to or even more unjust than the one that preceded it.

But maybe we want more than to play Whac-A-Mole with injustice. If we want to do more than alter the color of our children's chains, we will have to successfully oppose more than isolated instances of oppression. I suspect that this is why prison scholar Ruth Wilson Gilmore stressed that "abolition is about presence, not absence" and fellow abolitionist Micah Herskind called it "the dual-pronged project of tearing down and building up, the dismantling of life-sucking

systems alongside the construction of life-giving ones."[62]
Gilmore and Herskind also strike a similar chord with the anti-colonial ethos of PAIGC militant Amílcar Cabral, which, in the words of Kenyan activist Firoze Manji, can be summarized as "self-determination, not secession."[63]

A constructive approach to politics involves building power in and through institutions and networks. Some of these operate apart from or in the margins of the more dominant global institutions: like the collective informal economic and mutual aid practices that Black peoples and others have practiced continuously over the past centuries.[64] But many needed institutions are well known, tried-and-true engines of social progress. Labor unions allow workers to bargain collectively over their working conditions and compensation— pivotal struggles in and of themselves that decide the basic economic and social conditions of life for scores of people. But the political potential of unions is, of course, even more significant than this. Organized workers can use their leverage for goals far beyond wages and benefits, and historically have often done so.

In the United States, unions played a pivotal role in dismantling the Jim Crow system of formal segregation and developing the concept and practice of a "just transition" of workers out of environmentally and socially harmful industries into beneficial ones.[65] Correspondingly, it was a courageous strike by workers (and its violent repression by colonial police) that launched the PAIGC's successful anti-colonial struggle.[66] More recently, Egyptian, Algerian, and Kuwaiti trade unions have defied bans and repression to force concessions from the regimes whose abuses sparked the Arab Spring uprisings of 2011, as well as from the ones that followed it.[67]

Some of the other institutions we will have to build may be less familiar. In 2013, a coalition of organizers launched a crowd-funded "Rolling Jubilee" campaign to erase more than $30 million worth of medical, tuition, payday loan, and criminal debt for thousands of unaffiliated people. That coalition morphed into a debtors' union called the Debt Collective.

Student debt alone in the United States is worth $1.7 trillion—which, the Debt Collective points out, turns into $1.7 trillion worth of leverage on the global financial system if it is tightly organized.

Around the world, organizations fighting for housing justice, ranging from squatters' groups to tenants' unions, are challenging the dictates of capital over housing markets.[68] As the Debt Collective point outs, these old and new formations can be mutually supporting partners. An illustrative example is the successful revolt of the people of Cochabamba, Bolivia, against the privatization of the city's water system by US-based multinational Bechtel—a movement that employed a combination of general strikes and guerilla military tactics to preserve public control over the commons.[69]

But a constructive approach to politics calls for us to build power expansively, across all aspects of social life—beyond just work. This is especially important in the digital era. Among the threats posed by this most recent stage of racial capitalism are the erosion of the practical and material bases for popular power over knowledge production and distribution.

The capture and corruption of these bases by well-positioned elites, especially tech corporations, goes on unabated and largely unchallenged.

We are seeing the corporate monopolization of local news and social media, the ongoing destruction and looting of the journalistic profession, and the domination of elite interests in the production of knowledge by research universities and think tanks. But, as the long history of muckraking, abolitionist newspapers, consciousness raising, and political education campaigns shows, information networks aid effective political action and can constrain the system's violence. Many people are hard at work developing their twenty-first-century analogues, building strong networks for movement journalism, encouraging adoption of alternative social media platforms, and increasing the research capacity of left organizations. They deserve and need our support.

Rules and procedures can help keep these ventures stable and well directed. But *Robert's Rules of Order* cannot do much to constrain toxic organizing cultures. We will have to think more comprehensively.

In a speech describing social movements like the anti-imperialist struggles he was then fighting against the Portuguese Empire, Cabral observed that "national liberation is necessarily an act of culture."[70] By "culture," Cabral did not mean that a carefully curated list of customary greetings, traditional foods, and styles of dress were themselves going to bring down the military forces of a fascist empire.

Culture is "the vigorous manifestation on the ideological or idealist plane" of people and "a product of their history,"

Cabral observed. But he also insisted that culture is not just an idle ideological force or set of fashions and preferences that results from past and present trends; it is also "a determinant of history, by the positive or negative influence which it exerts on the evolution of relationships between man and his environment." This is why he claimed that imperialist domination "can be maintained only by the permanent, organized repression of the cultural life of the people concerned." After all, if people are in the habit of determining for themselves how to organize more of their lives than they are currently allowed to, cunning imperialists understand that the colonized might eventually go for the whole pie. In this sense, then, the struggle for national liberation was simply "the organized political expression of the culture of the people who are undertaking the struggle."[71] We should put our cultural norms to the same constructive test as our other goals and aspirations: "The important thing is to proceed to critical analysis of African cultures in relation to the liberation movement and to the exigencies of progress." That is, we should evaluate our culture instrumentally, by how well it helps us build what we are trying to build.[72]

A constructive political culture would focus on outcome over process—the pursuit of specific goals or end results rather than avoiding complicity in injustice or promoting purely moral or aesthetic principles.

When it comes to knowledge and information, we should be concerned primarily with building institutions and campaign-relevant practices of information gathering and sharing rather than centering specific groups of people or spokespeople who stand in for them. And we should calibrate our program directly to the task of redistributing social resources and power rather than to pedestals, attention, or symbolism.

We need to focus on building and rebuilding rooms, not on regulating traffic within and between them. This is a world-making project aimed at building and rebuilding actual structures of social connection and movement, not mere critique of the ones we already have.

We should set our sights on different scales, from local fights like community control over land, housing, and energy to global ones over debt cancellation in the global South. These fights, especially when they are planetary in scope, make it possible to totally revamp our global social system—to rebuild the house we all live in together.

5

The Point
Is to Change It

Writing in the 1880s, Karl Marx famously observed, "Philosophers have only interpreted the world, in various ways; the point, however, is to change it."[1] After all, no matter who we "center" in our organizing culture's thoughts and messages, there will be lead in our water until and unless we do something about the pipes.

Over a century later and an ocean away, Afro-Guyanese activist and intellectual Andaiye sounded a similar alarm: "Old foundations are crumbling," she warned, "and new ones are not yet being imagined."

I'm not alone in seeing an affinity between these lines of thinking: it was for good reason that Alissa Trotz, editor of the collection of Andaiye's essays in which I discovered this quote, gave the book the title *The Point Is to Change the World* and included Marx's eleventh thesis on Feuerbach as its epigraph.[2]

But while Marx's comment encapsulates the ancient struggle over the place of philosophy in any age, Andaiye's provokes us to examine its relevance in this one.

Andaiye was born on September 11, 1941, in George-town, the capital of what was then British Guiana. With the approval of President John F. Kennedy, the CIA conspired to rig the soon-to-be-independent country's elections, ousting the outspokenly Communist Indo-Guyanese Cheddi Jagan in favor of a perceived moderate, Forbes Burnham. His rule, which Guyanese historian Clem Seecharan characterizes as a dictatorship, would last for sixteen years.[3]

While her country descended into what Seecharan describes as a "virtual racial war between Africans and Indians," a young Andaiye was hard at work educating herself and deepening her radical politics. She studied at the University of the West Indies with fellow student and eventual comrade Walter Rodney, and later lectured in a program for "disadvantaged students" in the United States. She returned home with a staunch feminist and Marxist politics rooted in solidarity. Among her many Guya-nese organizational affiliations were the Red Thread women's organization and the Working People's Alliance.

By 2009, when she was invited to give a commencement speech at her alma mater, Andaiye was a veteran activist, deeply attuned to the stakes of political analysis. And when she observed that "old foundations are crumbling, and new ones are not yet being imagined," she was not talking about the structure of philosophical analysis or patterns of political discourse. She was talking about the weather.

Andaiye went on to explain that "old assumptions about weather patterns and how these shape major economic occu-pations are no longer valid."[4] Climate crises in the Caribbean were mounting. At the time, climate change might have seemed like a drop in the bucket in larger countries with advanced economies, but for the small island states of the Caribbean, it already posed an existential crisis. In 2005, her home country lost the equivalent of 60 percent of its gross domestic product in a single flood that covered a mere twenty-five miles of its more than two hundred–mile coastline.[5]

Such ecological crises are exacerbating long-standing forms of injustice in the world economy. For instance, after the flooding in Guyana, women caregivers and subsistence farmers shouldered massively increased burdens.

The North American Free Trade Agreement (NAFTA) likewise contributed to gender injustices. Women were shuffled out of sectors like manufacturing at rates more than double those of men, increasing their already-disproportionate representation in the precarious informal sector. Massive majorities of farming populations in Dominica were shunted out of the relatively secure formal sector into the informal sector. Racial violence increased in Guyana, police violence spiked in Jamaica, and domestic and sexual violence surged throughout the region.

Confronted by these crises, Andaiye said, such countries turned where they had to for funds: the International Monetary Fund. And they did so despite the fact that little had changed since the financial institution's disastrous structural adjustment policies of the 1970s.

In response, Andaiye called for imagination—not to more incisively describe the failures of the first or second wave of policies, but to overcome the lack of new solutions that forced the region back to familiar and available nonsolutions. She called for builders.

Andaiye was in good company. Abolitionist scholar Ruth Wilson Gilmore, in her classic book *Golden Gulag*, documents a deep irony of the rise of California's prison system, especially given US capitalism's long-standing anti-communism: its world historical levels of incarceration were built via tight coordination between corporations, bankers, and government officials—that is, "central planning." But Gilmore also noticed something about the successful resistance of California communities, including one in Tulane County, where family ranchers and farmworkers united under the banners of the United Farm Workers fought off a planned prison construction. Even without the "technocratic expertise" that the bankers and state government wielded, the community's activists put forward "alternate planning criteria that must precede any industrial location decision," which Gilmore calls "grassroots planning."[6]

Both Andaiye and Gilmore propose, then, that planning creates places. The question the constructive program asks is: Will the plans be theirs or ours?

What the Constructive Approach Asks of Us

The constructive approach to politics does not ask us to invent a political culture out of whole cloth. "Constructive" is just a name, after all. Many of the people who came before us, including those profiled in this book, practiced constructive politics without having any need of this particular word to describe what they were doing.

A constructive program does not ask us to ignore our own interpersonal, symbolic, or material needs, even though it does ask us to be disciplined in how we relate those to the needs of the struggle and of the scores of people and generations that are not immediately present. After reading the book *Woman Power* by Cellestine Ware, Demita Frazier of the Combahee River Collective recalls arriving at the view that it is both Black women's "right and responsibility" to analyze their social position as part of their radical perspective.[7] I think the rest of us should take a page from this book as well.

The constructive approach is, however, extremely demanding. It asks us to be planners and designers, to be accountable and responsive to people who aren't yet in the room. In addition to being architects, it asks us to become builders and construction workers: to actually build the kinds of rooms we could sit in together, rather than idly speculate about which rooms would be nice. But it's important to acknowledge, in closing this book, that the constructive approach has implicit moral and emotional demands, as well: we can neither plan nor build a better world without collectively cultivating diverse kinds of moral and emotional discipline.

The deferential approach to politics is worth praising because of its concern and attention to the importance of lived experience—especially traumatic experiences. But just as this virtue becomes a vice when "being in the room" effects are ignored, this virtue also becomes a vice when trauma's importance and prevalence are framed as positive bases for social credentials and deference behaviors, rather than primarily as problems to deal with collectively.

Here, scholarly analysis and argument fail me. The remainder of what I have to say skews more toward conviction than contention. But life has taught me that conviction has much to teach, however differently posed or processed, and so I press on.

I take concerns about trauma especially seriously. I grew up in the United States, a nation structured by settler colonialism, racial slavery, and their aftermath, with enough collective and historical trauma to go around. I also grew up in a Nigerian diasporic community, populated by many who had genocide in their living memory.

At the national and community level, I have seen personality traits, quirks of habit and action, that I've suspected were born of these grim parts of history. Like most people, I have not been spared. I've watched and felt myself change in reaction to fearing for my dignity or life, to crushing pain and humiliation. I reflect on these traumatic moments often, and very seldom do I think, "That was educational."

These experiences can be, if we are very fortunate, building blocks. What comes of them depends on how the blocks are put together. Those who study the politics of knowledge call this the "achievement thesis." As philosopher Briana Toole clarifies, by itself, one's social location only puts a person in a position to know; "epistemic privilege" or advantage, on the other hand, is achieved only through deliberate, concerted struggle from that position.[8]

Humiliation, deprivation, and suffering can build—especially in the context of the deliberate, structured effort of "consciousness raising" that Toole specifically highlights. But these same experiences can also destroy, and if I had to bet on which effect would win most often, it would be the latter.

Contra the old expression, pain, whether born of oppression or not, is a poor teacher. Suffering is partial, shortsighted, and self-absorbed. We shouldn't have a politics that expects different. Oppression is not a prep school.

Demanding as the constructive approach may be, the deferential approach is far more so, and in a far more unfair way. As philosopher Agnes Callard rightly notes, trauma (and even the righteous, well-deserved anger that often accompanies it) can corrupt as readily as it can ennoble.[9] Perhaps more so.

When it comes down to it, the thing I believe most deeply about deference politics is that it asks something of trauma that it cannot give. It asks the traumatized to shoulder burdens alone that we ought to share collectively, lifting them up onto a pedestal in order to hide below them.

When I think about my trauma, I don't think about life lessons. I think about the quiet nobility of survival. The very fact that those chapters weren't the final ones of my story is powerful enough all on its own. It is enough to ask of those experiences that I am still here to remember them.

I also believe that deference politics asks us to be less than we are—and not even for our own benefit. As scholar-activist Nick Estes explains in the context of Indigenous politics, "The cunning of trauma politics is that it turns actual people and struggles, whether racial or Indigenous citizenship and belonging, into matters of injury. It defines an entire people mostly on their trauma and not by their aspirations or sheer humanity." This performance is not for the benefit of Indigenous people; rather, "it's for white audiences or institutions of power."[10]

When I think about my trauma, I also think about the great writer James Baldwin's realization that the things that most tormented him "were the very things that connected me with all the people who were alive, or who had ever been alive."[11]

That I have experienced my share of traumatic experiences, have survived abuse of various kinds, have faced near death from accidental circumstance and from violence (different as the particulars of these may be from those around me) is not a card to play in gamified social interaction or a weapon to wield in battles over prestige. It is not what gives me a special right to speak, to evaluate, or to decide for a group. It is a concrete, experiential manifestation of the vulnerability that connects me to most of the people on this earth. It comes between me and other people not as a wall, but as a bridge.

Going together—the politics of solidarity, which deference provides one, flawed model of doing—is a good start. But on its own, it's not enough. We also have to decide collectively where we're going, and then we have to do what it takes to get there. Though we start from different levels of privilege or advantage, this journey is not a matter of figuring out who should bow to whom, but simply one of figuring out how best to join forces. As Paulo Freire showed us in theory, and the African anti-colonial and Portuguese Carnation revolutions showed us in practice, we will need each other to get where we're going. And getting there, after all, is the point.

Notes

Introduction

An earlier version of this essay appeared as "Identity Politics and Elite Capture," *Boston Review*, May 7, 2020, https://bostonreview.net/articles/olufemi-o-taiwo-identity-politics-and-elite-capture/.

1. Amílcar Cabral, *Unity and Struggle: Speeches and Writings of Amílcar Cabral*, vol. 3 (New York: New York University Press, 1979), 86.

2. Max Bearak and Rael Ombuor, "Kenyan Police Shot Dead a Teenager on His Balcony during a Coronavirus Curfew Crackdown," *Washington Post*, March 31, 2021, https://www.washingtonpost.com/world/africa/kenyan-police-shot-dead-a-teenager-on-his-balcony-during-a-coronavirus-curfew-crackdown/2020/03/31/6344c70e-7350-11ea-ad9b-254ec99993bc_story.html.

3. Jorge Valencia, "Black Lives Matter Protests Renew Parallel Debates in Brazil, Colombia," *The World*, June 15, 2021, https://www.pri.org/stories/2020-06-15/black-lives-matter-protests-renew-parallel-debates-brazil-colombia.

4. "Demonstrators in Brazil Protest against Crimes Committed by Police," *VOA News*, June 1, 2020, https://www.voanews.com/americas/demonstrators-brazil-protest-against-crimes-committed-police.

5. César Muñoz, "Brazil Suffers Its Own Scourge of Police Brutality," *Human Rights Watch*, June 3, 2020, https://www

.hrw.org/news/2020/06/03/brazil-suffers-its-own-scourge
-police-brutality.

6. "Rio Violence: Police Killings Reach Record High in 2019,"
   BBC News, January 23, 2020, https://www.bbc.com/news
   /world-latin-america-51220364.

7. Larry Buchanan, Quoctrung Bui, and Jugal K. Patel, "Black
   Lives Matter May Be the Largest Movement in U.S. History,"
   New York Times, July 3, 2020, https://www.nytimes.com
   /interactive/2020/07/03/us/george-floyd-protests-crowd-size
   .html; Dudley L. Poston Jr., "3 Ways That the U.S. Population
   Will Change over the Next Decade," *PBS NewsHour*, accessed
   January 2, 2020, https://www.pbs.org/newshour/nation
   /3-ways-that-the-u-s-population-will-change-over-the
   -next-decade.

8. Jen Kirby, "'Black Lives Matter' Has Become a Global Rally-
   ing Cry," *Vox*, June 12, 2020, https://www.vox.com
   /2020/6/12/21285244/black-lives-matter-global-protests
   -george-floyd-uk-belgium.

9. "Nigeria's Lekki Shooting: What Has Happened so Far at
   Lagos Judicial Panel," *BBC News*, November 27, 2020,
   https://www.bbc.com/news/world-africa-55099016.

10. I explore this question in greater depth in my book *Reconsid-
    ering Reparations: Worldmaking in the Case of Climate Crisis*
    (New York: Oxford University Press, 2021); Kwame Nkrumah,
    "Neo-Colonialism: The Last Stage of Imperialism," 1967; F
    Pigeaud and NS Sylla, "Africa's Last Colonial Currency: The
    CFA Franc Story," 2021.

11. David Malpass, "June 18, 2020: Ending Racism," *Voices*, June
    18, 2020, https://blogs.worldbank.org/voices/june-18-2020
    -ending-racism; Chris Cannito, "UN Human Rights Council
    Holds Historic Hearings on Racism in US," *Nonprofit Quarter-
    ly*, June 22, 2020, https://nonprofitquarterly.org/un-human
    -rights-council-holds-historic-hearings-on-racism-in-us/.

12. Roberto Lovato, "The Age of Intersectional Empire Is Upon Us," May 10, 2021, *The Nation*, https://www.thenation.com/article/politics/cia-video-intersectional/.

13. Talia Lavin, "The 1960s Previewed the GOP Attack on 'Critical Race Theory,'" *MSNBC*, June 22, 2021, https://www.msnbc.com/opinion/right-wing-freakout-about-critical-race-theory-began-1960s-n1271670; Kevin M. Kruse, "The Trump Administration's Thinly-Veiled Rebuke of 'The 1619 Project' is a Sloppy, Racist Mess," *MSNBC*, accessed January 20, 2021, https://www.msnbc.com/opinion/trump-administration-s-thinly-veiled-rebuke-1619-project-sloppy-racist-n1254807.

14. Amy Cassidy and Tara John, "UN Condemns 'Reprehensible' UK Race Report for Repackaging 'Racist Tropes into Fact,'" *CNN*, April 19, 2021, https://www.cnn.com/2021/04/19/uk/un-uk-race-report-intl-gbr/index.html; Tara John, "Analysis: Culture Wars Give Boris Johnson and His Government a Quick and Easy High. They're No Substitute for Governing," *CNN*, accessed April 4, 2021, https://www.cnn.com/2021/04/04/uk/uk-race-report-culture-wars-intl-gbr/index.html.

15. Ashley Bohrer, "Intersectionality and Marxism: A Critical Historiography," *Historical Materialism* 26, no. 2 (2018): 60.

16. Dominic Gustavo, "'Humans of CIA' Recruitment Campaign Sells Youth 'Identity Politics Imperialism,'" *World Socialist Web Site*, May 20, 2021, https://www.wsws.org/en/articles/2021/05/20/ciar-m20.html.

17. Duchess Harris, "From the Kennedy Commission to the Combahee Collective," in *Sisters in the Struggle* (New York: New York University Press, 2001), 280–305.

18. Harris, "Combahee Collective," 280–305.

19. Keeanga-Yamahtta Taylor, *How We Get Free: Black Feminism and the Combahee River Collective* (Chicago: Haymarket Books, 2017), 5–6 (my emphasis).

20. Terrell Jermaine Starr, "Barbara Smith, Who Helped Coin the Term 'Identity Politics,' Endorses Bernie Sanders," *The Root*, accessed February 3, 2020, https://www.theroot.com/barbara-smith-who-helped-coin-the-term-identity-politi-1841419291; Barbara Smith, "I Helped Coin the Term 'Identity Politics'. I'm Endorsing Bernie Sanders," *Guardian*, February 10, 2020, http://www.theguardian.com/commentisfree/2020/feb/10/identity-politics-bernie-sanders-endorsement.

21. Taylor, *How We Get Free*, 107–9.

22. Starr, "Barbara Smith Endorses Bernie Sanders."

23. Asad Haider, "Identity Politics," chapter 1 in *Mistaken Identity: Race and Class in the Age of Trump* (Verso Books, 2018), 7–26.

24. Marie Moran, "(Un) Troubling Identity Politics: A Cultural Materialist Intervention," *European Journal of Social Theory* 23, no. 2 (2020): 258–77; Linda Martín Alcoff, "The Political Critique," chapter 2 in *Visible Identities: Race, Gender, and the Self* (Oxford University Press, 2005), 20–46.

25. Tess Bonn, "Saagar Enjeti Laments Use of Identity Politics in 2020 Democratic Race," *The Hill*, November 26, 2019, https://thehill.com/hilltv/rising/472191-saagar-enjeti-laments-use-of-identity-politics-in-2020-democratic-race.

26. Michael C. Dawson, *Blacks in and out of the Left* (Cambridge, MA: Harvard University Press, 2013), 194.

27. Adom Getachew, *Worldmaking after Empire: The Rise and Fall of Self-Determination* (Princeton, NJ: Princeton University Press, 2019).

Chapter 1: What Is Elite Capture?

1. Tony Platt, "E. Franklin Frazier Reconsidered," *Social Justice* 16, no. 4 (1989): 186–95; Malik Simba, "E. Franklin Frazier (1894–1962)," *Black Past*, January 19, 2007, https://www.blackpast.org

/african-american-history/frazier-e-franklin-1894-1962/; Arthur P. Davis, "E. Franklin Frazier (1894–1962): A Profile," *Journal of Negro Education* 31, no. 4 (1962): 429–35.

2. Tony Platt and Susan Chandler, "Constant Struggle: E. Franklin Frazier and Black Social Work in the 1920s," *Social Work* 33, no. 4 (1988): 293–97.

3. Frazier's 1939 book *The Negro Family in the United States* was a widely acclaimed sociological account of Black American life. See Randal Maurice Jelks and Ayesha K. Hardison, "Black Love after E. Franklin Frazier: An Introduction," *Women, Gender, and Families of Color* 7, no. 2 (2019): 108–12.

4. Lori Martin, "Africana Demography: Lessons from Founders E. Franklin Frazier, WEB Du Bois, and the Atlanta School of Sociology," *Issues in Race and Society* 8 (2019): 5–28; Earl Wright and Thomas C. Calhoun, "Jim Crow Sociology: Toward an Understanding of the Origin and Principles of Black Sociology via the Atlanta Sociological Laboratory," *Sociological Focus* 39, no. 1 (2006): 1–18.

5. Frantz Fanon, *The Wretched of the Earth*, Constance Farrington, trans. (New York: Grove, 1963), 149–51.

6. Fanon, *Wretched of the Earth*, 148.

7. Fanon, "The Trials and Tribulations of National Consciousness," chapter 3 in *The Wretched of the Earth* (1961), Richard Philcox, trans. (New York: Grove, 2004), 97–144.

8. Kwame Nkrumah, *Neo-Colonialism: The Last Stage of Imperialism* (New York: International Publishers, 1966).

9. Bernard Magubane and Nzongola-Ntalaja, *Proletarianization and Class Struggle in Africa* (San Francisco: Synthesis Publications, n.d.), 57.

10. Fanon, *Wretched of the Earth* (2004 ed.), 97–144.

11. E. Franklin Frazier, *Black Bourgeoisie* (New York: Free Press, 1997), 104.

12. Frazier, "Negro Business: A Social Myth," chapter 7 in *Black*

Bourgeoisie, 153–73.

13. Frazier, *Black Bourgeoisie*, 235.

14. Frazier, *Black Bourgeoisie*, 236.

15. Jared A. Ball, *The Myth and Propaganda of Black Buying Power* (New York: Springer, 2020).

16. Ball, "Introduction" in *Black Buying Power*, 1–10.

17. Jo Freeman, "The Tyranny of Stucturelessness," Jo Freeman official website, https://www.jofreeman.com/joreen/tyranny.htm.

18. For examples, see Monica Martinez-Bravo, Priya Mukherjee, and Andreas Stegmann, "The Non-democratic Roots of Elite Capture: Evidence from Soeharto Mayors in Indonesia," *Econometrica* 85, no. 6 (2017): 1991–2010; Pranab K. Bardhan and Dilip Mookherjee, "Capture and Governance at Local and National Levels," *American Economic Review* 90, no. 2 (2000): 135–39; Daron Acemoglu and James A. Robinson, "Persistence of Power, Elites, and Institutions," *American Economic Review* 98, no. 1 (2008): 267–93.

19. Diya Dutta, "Elite Capture and Corruption: Concepts and Definitions," *National Council of Applied Economic Research*, 2009, 4.

20. Dutta, "Elite Capture and Corruption," 5.

21. Wendy Brown, "Neo-Liberalism and the End of Liberal Democracy," *Theory and Event* 7, no. 1 (2003); Tyler Stovall, *White Freedom: The Racial History of an Idea* (Princeton, NJ: Princeton University Press, 2021).

22. Keeanga-Yamahtta Taylor, *From#BlackLivesMatter to Black Liberation* (Chicago: Haymarket Books, 2016), 100.

23. Cited in David Farber, *Crack: Rock Cocaine, Street Capitalism, and the Decade of Greed* (Cambridge, UK: Cambridge University Press, 2019), 144.

24. Ryan Devereaux, "How the CIA Watched Over the Destruction of Gary Webb," *The Intercept*, September 25, 2014, https://theintercept.com/2014/09/25/managing-nightmare -cia-media-destruction-gary-webb/.

25. Neil Fligstein and Linda Markowitz, "Financial Reorganization of American Corporations in the 1980s," *Sociology and the Public Agenda*, 1993, 185–206; Neil Fligstein and Taek-Jin Shin, "The Shareholder Value Society: A Review of the Changes in Working Conditions and Inequality in the United States, 1976 to 2000," *Social Inequality*, 2004, 401–32; Samuel Knafo and Sahil Jai Dutta, "The Myth of the Shareholder Revolution and the Financialization of the Firm," *Review of International Political Economy* 27, no. 3 (2020): 476–99; Peter Nolan, Jin Zhang, and Chunhang Liu, "The Global Business Revolution, the Cascade Effect, and the Challenge for Firms from Developing Countries," *Cambridge Journal of Economics* 32, no. 1 (2008): 42–43.

26. Doug Henwood, "Take Me to Your Leader: The Rot of the American Ruling Class," *Jacobin*, April 27, 2021, https://jacobinmag.com/2021/04/take-me-to-your-leader-the-rot-of-the-american-ruling-class.

27. Knafo and Dutta argue, alongside an earlier analysis by Fligstein and against much of the existing literature, that the 80s shareholder revolution was one phase in a longer arc of major changes in corporate governance. The quote in this section is from Nolan, Zhang, and Liu's analysis. Knafo and Dutta, "The Myth of the Shareholder Revolution and the Financialization of the Firm"; Nolan, Zhang, and Liu, "The Global Business Revolution, the Cascade Effect, and the Challenge for Firms from Developing Countries," 43.

28. Benjamin P. Edwards, "Arbitration's Dark Shadow," *Nev. LJ* 18 (2017): 427.

29. Daniela Gabor and Ndongo Samba Sylla, "Planting Budgetary Time Bombs in Africa: The Macron Doctrine En Marche," CADTM, September 18, 2021, https://www.cadtm.org/Planting-budgetary-time-bombs-in-Africa-the-Macron-Doctrine-En-Marche.

30. Karen Hao, "Troll Farms Reached 140 Million Americans a

Month on Facebook before 2020 Election, Internal Report Shows," *MIT Technology Review*, September 16, 2021, https://www.technologyreview.com/2021/09/16/1035851/facebook-troll-farms-report-us-2020-election/.

31. Daniel Tetteh Osabu-Kle, "The Politics of One-Sided Adjustment in Africa," *Journal of Black Studies* 30, no. 4 (2000): 515–33; Jason Hickel, "Apartheid in the World Bank and the IMF," *Al Jazeera*, November 26, 2020, https://www.aljazeera.com/opinions/2020/11/26/it-is-time-to-decolonise-the-world-bank-and-the-imf; Ngaire Woods, "Unelected Government: Making the IMF and the World Bank More Accountable," *Brookings* (blog), April 1, 2003 https://www.brookings.edu/articles/unelected-government-making-the-imf-and-the-world-bank-more-accountable/.

32. York W. Bradshaw and Jie Huang, "Intensifying Global Dependency: Foreign Debt, Structural Adjustment, and Third World Underdevelopment," *Sociological Quarterly* 32, no. 3 (1991): 321–42; Issa G. Shivji, "Samir Amin on Democracy and Fascism," *Agrarian South: Journal of Political Economy* 9, no. 1 (2020): 12–32.

33. Keston Perry, "Realising Climate Reparations: Towards a Global Climate Stabilization Fund and Resilience Fund Programme for Loss and Damage in Marginalised and Former Colonised Societies," *Social Science Research Network*, 2020.

34. Hickel, "Apartheid in the World Bank and the IMF."

35. Thea Riofrancos, *Resource Radicals: From Petro-nationalism to Post-extractivism in Ecuador* (Durham, NC: Duke University Press, 2020).

36. Shivji, "Samir Amin on Democracy and Fascism," 13.

37. Wolfgang Streeck, *How Will Capitalism End?: Essays on a Failing System* (London and New York: Verso, 2016), 20.

38. Stephen Ferguson, *Philosophy of African American Studies: Nothing Left of Blackness* (New York: Springer, 2015), 36.

39. Angela Yvonne Davis, "The Anti-slavery Movement and the Birth of Women's Rights," chapter 2 and "Class and Race in the Early Women's Rights Campaign," chapter 3 in *Women, Race, and Class* (New York: Vintage, 1983), 30–69.

40. This allegation is perhaps most famously made by Angela Davis in *Women, Race, and Class* but has been debated in the decades since. For an analysis tying Frazier's account to patriarchy, see Curwood; for a defense of Frazier, see Semmes. Davis, 14; Anastasia Curwood, "A FRESH LOOK AT E. FRANKLIN FRAZIER'S SEXUAL POLITICS IN THE NEGRO FAMILY IN THE UNITED STATES," *Du Bois Review: Social Science Research on Race* 5, no. 2 (2008): 325–37, https://doi.org/10.1017/S1742058X08080193; Clovis E. Semmes, "E. Franklin Frazier's Theory of the Black Family: Vindication and Sociological Insight," *J. Soc. & Soc. Welfare* 28, no. 2 (2001): 3.

41. Dawson, *Blacks in and out of the Left*.

42. Shannon Keating, "You Wanted Same-Sex Marriage? Now You Have Pete Buttigieg," *BuzzFeed News*, December 11, 2019, https://www.buzzfeednews.com/article/shannonkeating/pete-buttigieg-marriage-equality-lgbtq-gay-rights.

43. Barbara Smith, "Barbara Smith: Why I Left the Mainstream Queer Rights Movement," *New York Times*, June 19, 2019, https://www.nytimes.com/2019/06/19/us/barbara-smith-black-queer-rights.html.

Chapter 2: Reading the Room

1. Robert F. Durden, "In the Shadow of Slavery," *The Life of Carter G. Woodson: Father of African-American History* (New York: Enslow Publishers), 8–19.

2. Durden, *Life of Carter G. Woodson*, 8–19.

3. Durden, *Life of Carter G. Woodson*, 8–19; W. E. B. Du Bois, *Black Reconstruction in America: Toward a History of the Part Which Black Folk Played in the Attempt to Reconstruct Democracy in America, 1860–1880* (New York: Harcourt Brace, 1935); Guy Emerson Mount, "When Slaves Go on Strike: W.E.B. Du Bois's Black Reconstruction 80 Years Later," *Black Perspectives*, December 28, 2015,"https://www.aaihs.org/when-slaves-go-on-strike/.

4. Jarvis R. Givens, "Fugitive Pedagogy," in *Fugitive Pedagogy* (Cambridge, MA: Harvard University Press, 2021), 4.

5. Durden, "Student, Teacher, Traveler," chapter 3 in *Life of Carter G. Woodson*, 20–25.

6. Durden, *Life of Carter G. Woodson*, 20–25.

7. "Key Events in Black Higher Education," *Journal of Blacks in Higher Education* official website, n.d., https://www.jbhe.com/chronology/.

8. Durden, "Launching Negro History Week, chapter 6 in *Life of Carter G. Woodson*, 47–63; Robert F. Schwarzwalder, Jr., "Francis J. Grimke: Prophet of Racial Justice, Skeptic of American Power," excerpt (PhD diss., University of Aberdeen, 2021), accessed at Regent University Library Link (blog) on March 21, 2021, http://digitallibrary.regent.edu/wordpress/?p=3546.

9. Daryl Michael Scott, "The History of Black History Month," *Black Past*, January 14, 2010, https://www.blackpast.org/african-american-history/history-black-history-month/.

10. Givens, "Fugitive Pedagogy."

11. Scott, "The History of Black History Month."

12. This term is Herb Clark's; see his *Using Language* (Cambridge, UK: Cambridge University Press, 1996).

13. Robert Stalnaker, *Context* (Oxford: Oxford University Press, 1966), 68, 78.

14. Robert Stalnaker, "Common Ground," *Linguistics and Philoso-*

phy 25 (2002): 701–21; Stalnaker, *Context*.

15. See Olúfẹ́mi O. Táíwò, "The Empire Has No Clothes," *Disputatio* 51 (2018): 305–30.

16. Kelly F. Austin, "Degradation and Disease: Ecologically Unequal Exchanges Cultivate Emerging Pandemics," *World Development* 137 (2021): 105–63; J. L. Austin, "Performative Utterances," in *Philosophical Papers*, J. O. Urmson and G. J. Warnock eds. (Oxford: Clarendon Press, 1961); Rebecca Kukla and Mark Norris Lance, *"Yo!'and'Lo!": The Pragmatic Topography of the Space of Reasons* (Cambridge, MA: Harvard University Press, 2009).

17. David Lewis, "Scorekeeping in a Language Game," *Journal of Philosophical Logic* 8, no. 1 (1979).

18. Lewis, "Scorekeeping in a Language Game," 340.

19. Miranda Fricker, *Epistemic Injustice: Power and the Ethics of Knowing* (Oxford: Oxford University Press, 2007).

20. Tommie Shelby, "Ideology, Racism, and Critical Social Theory," *Philosophical Forum* 34, no. 2 (2003): 153–88.

21. Robin D. G. Kelley, "' We Are Not What We Seem': Rethinking Black Working-Class Opposition in the Jim Crow South" *Journal of American History* 80, no. 7 (1993): 75–112; James C. Scott, *Domination and the Arts of Resistance: Hidden Transcripts* (New Haven: Yale University Press, 1990).

22. Gerald Vizenor, *Shadow Distance: A Gerald Vizenor Reader* (Middletown, CT: Wesleyan University Press, 1994); Goran Gumze, "Capoeira: Influences on Depression, Aggression and Violence in Salvador," (Ph.D diss., University of Nova Gorica, 2014) 32.

23. Carol Hanisch, "The Personal Is Political," February 1969, carolhanisch.org.

24. Carter G. Woodson, *The Mis-Education of the Negro* (Middletown, CT: Tribeca Books, 2016), 4.

25. Woodson, "How We Drifted Away from the Truth," chapter

3 in *Mis-Education of the Negro*

26. C. Thi Nguyen, "Layers of Agency," chapter 3 and "Gamification and Value Capture," chapter 9 in *Games: Agency as Art* (Oxford: Oxford University Press, 2018), 52–73, 189–215.

27. Noam Scheiber, "How Uber Uses Psychological Tricks to Push Its Drivers' Buttons," *New York Times*, April 2, 2017, https://www.nytimes.com/interactive/2017/04/02/technology/uber-drivers-psychological-tricks.html.

28. John Holden, "Big Companies Get Involved in Big Brother-Style Monitoring of Staff," *Irish Times*, August 18, 2014, https://www.irishtimes.com/business/big-companies-get-involved-in-big-brother-style-monitoring-of-staff-1.1898170; Sara Ashley O'Brien, "Workers at Amazon Brace for Another Grueling Week Spurred by Prime Day," *CNN*, June 21, 2021, https://www.cnn.com/2021/06/21/tech/workers-amazon-prime-day/index.html.

29. Nguyen, "Gamification and Value Capture," chapter 9 in *Games: Agency as Art*, 189–215.

30. Lewis, "Scorekeeping in a Language Game," 344–46.

31. Abigail Higgins and Olúfẹ́mi O. Táíwò, "Enforcing Eviction," *The Nation*, August 20, 2020, www.thenation.com/article/society/police-eviction-housing.

32. See Elizabeth Anderson, *Private Government: How Employers Rule Our Lives (and Why We Don't Talk about It)* (Princeton, NJ: Princeton University Press, 2017).

33. Arlie Russell Hochschild, *The Managed Heart: Commercialization of Human Feeling* (Berkeley: University of California Press, 1979).

34. Molly Jackman, "ALEC's Influence over Lawmaking in State Legislatures," *Brookings* (blog), December 6, 2013, www.brookings.edu/articles/alecs-influence-over-lawmaking-in-state-legislatures; Alexander C. Kaufman, "4 More States Propose Harsh New Penalties For Protesting Fossil Fuels,

HuffPost, February 20, 2021, www.huffpost.com/entry
/fossil-fuel-protest_n_602c1ff6c5b6c95056f3f6af; Alexander
C. Kaufman, "Yet Another State Quietly Moves to Crimi-
nalize Fossil Fuel Protests Amid Coronavirus," May 8, 2020,
www.huffpost.com/entry/alabama-fossil-fuel-pipeline
-protest-criminalize_n_5eb590b4c5b6197b8461d550.

35. George J. Stigler, "The Theory of Economic Regulation" *Bell
Journal of Management Science* 2, no. 1 (1971): 3–21; Ernesto
Dal Bó, "Regulatory Capture: A Review," *Oxford Review of
Economic Policy* 22, no. 2 (2006): 203–225.

36. "Shell Sued in UK for 'Decades of Oil Spills' in Nigeria," *Al
Jazeera*, November 22, 2016, www.aljazeera.com/news
/2016/11/22/shell-sued-in-uk-for-decades-of-oil-spills-in
-nigeria; Ike Okonta and Oronto Douglas, *Where Vultures
Feast: Shell, Human Rights, and Oil in the Niger Delta* (London
and New York: Verso, 2001).

37. Enegide Chinedu and Chukwuma Kelechukwu Chukwuemeka, "Oil Spillage and Heavy Metals Toxicity Risk in the
Niger Delta, Nigeria"; Noah, A.O., Adhikari, P., Ogundele,
B.O. and Yazdifar, H. (2021), "Corporate environmental
accountability in Nigeria: an example of regulatory failure
and regulatory capture," *Journal of Accounting in Emerging
Economies* 11, no. 1, https://doi.org/10.1108/JAEE-02-2019
-0038, 70–93; Bukola Adebayo, "Major New Inquiry into
Oil Spills in Niger Delta Launched," CNN, March 26, 2019,
https://www.cnn.com/2019/03/26/africa/nigeria-oil-spill-in
quiry-intl/index.html.

38. Davide Calenda and Albert Meijer, "Political Individualiza-
tion: New Media as an Escape from Family Control over
Political Behavior," *Information, Communication & Society* 14,
no. 5 (2011): 660–83.

39. Woodson, *Mis-Education of the Negro*, 20–21.

40. Saray Ayala, "Speech Affordances: A Structural Take on How

Much We Can Do with Our Words," *European Journal of Philosophy* 24, no. 4 (2016): 879–91; Táíwò, "Empire Has No Clothes."

41. Ayala, "Speech Affordances"; Kristie Dotson, "Conceptualizing Epistemic Oppression," *Social Epistemology*, 2014.

42. See Kukla and Lance, *"Yo!'and'Lo!"*

Chapter 3: Being in the Room

An earlier version of this essay appeared as "Being-in-the-Room Privilege: Elite Capture and Epistemic Difference," *The Philosopher* vol. 108, no. 4, https://www.thephilosopher1923.org/essay-taiwo.

1. Walter Rodney, *How Europe Underdeveloped Africa* (London and Dar Es Salaam: Bogle-L'Ouverture Publications, 1972).

2. Amílcar Cabral, *Return to the Source: Selected Speeches of Amílcar Cabral* (New York: Monthly Review Press, 1973), 51.

3. George E. Brooks, "Cabo Verde: Gulag of the South Atlantic: Racism, Fishing Prohibitions, and Famines," *History in Africa* 33 (2006): 101, https://doi.org/10.1353/hia.2006.0008.

4. Lilica Boal, "Mulheres de Abril: Testemunho de Lilica Boal," *Esquerda*, November 24, 2019, https://www.esquerda.net /artigo/mulheres-de-abril-testemunho-de-lilica-boal/64575.

5. Brooks, "Cabo Verde," 134.

6. Brooks, "Cabo Verde," 107, 111.

7. Brooks, "Cabo Verde," 107.

8. Brooks, "Cabo Verde," 107–11.

9. Alexander Keese, "Managing the Prospect of Famine: Cape Verdean Officials, Subsistence Emergencies, and the Change of Elite Attitudes During Portugal's Late Colonial Phase, 1939–1961," *Itinerario* 36, no. 1 (2012): 51.

10. Boal, "Mulheres de Abril."

11. Boal, "Mulheres de Abril."

12. Boal, "Mulheres de Abril."

13. Boal, "Mulheres de Abril."

14. Boal, "Mulheres de Abril."

15. Boal, "Mulheres de Abril."

16. Boal, "Mulheres de Abril"; António Tomás, *Amílcar Cabral: The Life of a Reluctant Nationalist* (London: Hurst & Co., 2021), 127–28.

17. World Health Organization, "1 in 3 People Globally Do Not Have Access to Safe Drinking Water – UNICEF, WHO," news release, June 18, 2021, https://www.who.int/news/item /18-06-2019-1-in-3-people-globally-do-not-have-access-to -safe-drinking-water-unicef-who; United Nations, "Affordable Housing Key for Development and Social Equality, UN Says on World Habitat Day," October 2, 2017, https://news. un.org/en/story/2017/10/567552-affordable-housing-key -development-and-social-equality-un-says-world-habitat.

18. Briana Toole, "Demarginalizing Standpoint Epistemology," *Episteme* 1 (2020): 19; Briana Toole, "From Standpoint Epistemology to Epistemic Oppression," *Hypatia* 34, no. 4 (2019): 598–618; Internet Encyclopedia of Philosophy, "Feminist Standpoint Theory," *Internet Encyclopedia of Philosophy*, https://iep.utm.edu/fem-stan/.

19. Liam Kofi Bright, "Empiricism Is a Standpoint Epistemology," *The Sooty Empiric* (blog), June 2018, https://sootyempiric .blogspot.com/2018/06/empiricism-is-standpoint -epistemology.html.

20. Priscilla Frank, "Touching Animation Recounts Story of Obama's 'Fired Up, Ready To Go' Chant," *HuffPost*, January 19, 2017, https://www.huffpost.com/entry/animated -film-obama-fired-up_n_5880ebd4e4b0e3a73567767e; Byron Tau, "The Story of 'Fired up! Ready to Go,'" *Politico*, April 4, 2012, https://www.politico.com/blogs/politico44/2012/04 /the-story-of-fired-up-ready-to-go-119612; Jeff Zeleny and Michael M. Grynbaum, "Obama Wins South Carolina Pri-

mary," *New York Times*, January 26, 2008, https://www
.nytimes.com/2008/01/26/us/politics/26cnd-carolina.html.

21. "Fired Up? Ready to Go?," White House official website, September 13, 2009, available at https://obamawhitehouse.archives
.gov/blog/2009/09/13/fired-ready-go.

22. Jo Freeman, "The Tyranny of Stucturelessness," Jo Freeman official website, https://www.jofreeman.com/joreen/tyranny.htm.

23. Freeman, "Tyranny of Stucturelessness."

24. Stephen Rohde, "The United States—A Model for the Nazis," *Los Angeles Review of Books*, September 3, 2017, https://
lareviewofbooks.org/article/the-united-states-a-model-for
-the-nazis/; James Q. Whitman, *Hitler's American Model: The United States and the Making of Nazi Race Law* (Princeton, NJ: Princeton University Press, 2017).

25. "Forty Percent of Nigerians Live below the Poverty Line: Report," *Al Jazeera*, May 4, 2020, https://www.aljazeera.com
/economy/2020/5/4/forty-percent-of-nigerians-live-below
-the-poverty-line-report; "The Most Successful Ethnic Group in the U.S. May Surprise You," *OZY*, January 6, 2018, https://www.ozy.com/around-the-world/the-most-successful
-ethnic-group-in-the-u-s-may-surprise-you/86885/; Leslie Casimir, "Data Show Nigerians the Most Educated in the U.S.," *Chron*, May 20, 2008, https://www.chron.com/news
/article/Data-show-Nigerians-the-most-educated-in-the
-U-S-1600808.php.

26. See Olúfémi O. Táíwò, "Being-in-the-Room Privilege: Elite Capture and Epistemic Deference," *The Philosopher* 108, no. 4 (2020).

27. Robert K Merton, "The Matthew Effect in Science: The Reward and Communication Systems of Science Are Considered," *Science* 159, no. 3810 (1968): 56–63; Paul D Allison, J Scott Long, and Tad K Krauze, "Cumulative Advantage and Inequality in Science," *American Sociological Review*, 1982, 615–25; Robert J

Sampson and John H Laub, "A Life-Course Theory of Cumulative Disadvantage and the Stability of Delinquency," *Developmental Theories of Crime and Delinquency* 7 (1997): 133–61.

28. Cabral, "National Liberation and Culture," Transition, no. 45 (1974): 12–17.

29. Cabral, "National Liberation and Culture."

Chapter 4: Building a New House

1. Amílcar Cabral, *Análise de Alguns Tipos de Resistência, Edição Do PAIGC* (Bolama: Guiné-Bissau Imprensa Nacional, 1979), my translation, available at http://www.cd25a.uc.pt/media /pdf/Biblioteca%20digital/Nreg%200715_%20Amilcar%20 Cabral_Analise%20se%20alguns%20tipos%20de%20 resistencia.pdf.

2. Paulo Freire, *Pedagogy of the Oppressed: 30th Anniversary*, M. B. Ramos, trans. (New York: Continuum, 1970), 30.

3. Paulo Freire, *Letters to Cristina* (London: Routledge, 2016), 21.

4. Freire, *Letters to Cristina*, 21.

5. Freire, *Pedagogy of the Oppressed*, 35; Anthony W. Pereira, "The US Role in the 1964 Coup in Brazil: A Reassessment," *Bulletin of Latin American Research* 37, no. 1 (2018): 5–17.

6. Freire, chapter 2 in *Pedagogy of the Oppressed*, 71–86.

7. Freire, *Pedagogy of the Oppressed*, 74–76.

8. Francisco J. Beltrán Tapia et al., "A Brief History of the Reconquista (718–1492 AD): Conquest, Repopulation and Land Distribution," *Documentos de Trabajo de la Sociedad Española de Historia Agraria*, 2004.

9. Peter Karibe Mendy, *Amílcar Cabral: A Nationalist and Pan-Africanist Revolutionary* (Athens: Ohio University Press, 2019), 24–28, 37.

10. Peter Karibe Mendy, "Portugal's Civilizing Mission in

Colonial Guinea-Bissau: Rhetoric and Reality," *International Journal of African Historical Studies* 36, no. 1 (2003): 35–58.

11. Mendy, *Amílcar Cabral*, 24–28.

12. Mendy, *Amílcar Cabral*, 29.

13. Mendy, *Amílcar Cabral*, 33.

14. Luís Reis Torgal, "Estado, Ideologia e História de Portugal," *Revista de História* 8 (1988): 345–55.

15. Stephanie Urdang, "Fighting Two Colonialisms: The Women's Struggle in Guinea-Bissau," *African Studies Review* 18, no. 3 (1975): 29.

16. Sónia Vaz Borges, *Militant Education, Liberation Struggle, Consciousness: The PAIGC Education in Guinea-Bissau 1963–1978* (Berlin: Peter Lang, 2019).

17. Vaz Borges, "The PAIGC's Freedom Fighter. The Process of Becoming Conscious and a Militant (1940's-1972)," *Militant Education*, 23–53.

18. Vaz Borges, *Militant Education*, 25.

19. Vaz Borges, *Militant Education*, 119.

20. Vaz Borges, *Militant Education*, 126.

21. Vaz Borges, "Building and Organizing Educational Structures in Guinea Bissau (1963-1972)," *Militant Education*, 53–98.

22. R. A. Akindele, "Africa and the Great Powers, with Particular Reference to the United States, the Soviet Union and China," *Africa Spectrum*, 1985, 125–51; Julião Soares Sousa, "Amílcar Cabral, the PAIGC and the Relations with China at the Time of the Sino-Soviet Split and of Anti-colonialism: Discourses and Praxis," *International History Review* 42, no. 6 (2020): 1274–96; Catarina Laranjeiro, "The Cuban Revolution and the Liberation Struggle in Guinea-Bissau: Images, Imaginings, Expectations and Experiences," *International History Review* 42, no. 6 (2020): 1319–38.

23. Suzanne Lipinska, "Two Weeks With the Guinea-Bissau Liberation Army," in *Cinéma Chez Les Balantes*, trans. Caroline

Higgitt (Ghent: KIOSK, 2014), 40.

24. Vaz Borges, *Militant Education*, 125; Lilica Boal, "Mulheres de Abril: Testemunho de Lilica Boal," *Esquerda*, November 24, 2019, https://www.esquerda.net/artigo/mulheres-de-abril-testemunho-de-lilica-boal/64575.

25. Vaz Borges, *Militant Education*, 66.

26. Vaz Borges, *Militant Education*, 62–65.

27. Urdang, "Fighting Two Colonialisms," 30.

28. Urdang, "Fighting Two Colonialisms," 30.

29. Lipinska, "Two Weeks with the Guinea-Bissau Liberation Army," 9.

30. Vaz Borges, *Militant Education*, 163.

31. Vaz Borges, *Militant Education*, 164–66.

32. Marina Padrão Temudo and Manuel Bivar Abrantes, "Changing Policies, Shifting Livelihoods: The Fate of Agriculture in Guinea-Bissau," *Journal of Agrarian Change* 13, no. 4 (2013): 575.

33. António Tomás, *Amílcar Cabral: The Life of a Reluctant Nationalist* (London: Hurst & Co., 2021), 127.

34. Maria do Carmo Rebouças da Cruz and Ferreira dos Santos, "A Recolonização de Guiné-Bissau Por Meio Das Representações Negativas Realizadas Pelos Organismos Internacionais de Desenvolvimento: De 'Estado Frágil' a 'Narco-Estado,'" *Desenvolvimento Em Questão* 17, no. 47 (2019): 156–78; Tomás, *Amílcar Cabral.*

35. Thomas C. Bruneau, "The Guinea-Bissau Case" in *Security Forces in African States*, Paula Shmella and Nicholas Tomb, ed (Amherst, NY: Cambria Press, 2017).

36. Julião Soares Sousa, "Prefácio," in *Por Uma Reinvenção Da Governabilidade e Do Equilíbrio de Poder Na Guiné-Bissau: Diálogos e Olhares Cruzado a Partir Da Diáspora* (Middletown, CT: independently published, 2014), 3–4.

37. Mark Shaw, "Drug Trafficking in Guinea-Bissau, 1998–2014: The Evolution of an Elite Protection Network," *Journal of*

Modern African Studies 53, no. 3 (2015): 339–64; Emmanuel Uzuegbu-Wilson, "A Critical Review of Evolutionary Trends of Drug Trafficking in Guinea-Bissau," *Social Science Research Network*, 2019.

38. "Is Cape Verde Doomed to Become a Narco-State?," *ENACT Africa*, June 4, 2019, https://enactafrica.org/enact-observer/is-cape-verde-doomed-to-become-a-narco-state; Colin Free-man, "The Cocaine Highway: On the Front Line of Europe's Drug War," *Telegraph*, November 3, 2019, https://www.telegraph.co.uk/news/drug-trafficking-in-cape-verde/.

39. Ashley Neese Bybee, *Narco State or Failed State? Narcotics and Politics in Guinea-Bissau* (Fairfax, VA: George Mason University Press, 2011); Sonia Pires, "Guinea-Bissau Immigrant Transnationalism in Portugal: A Substitute for a Failed State?," *African and Black Diaspora: An International Journal* 6, no. 2 (2013): 145–73.

40. "Guinea-Bissau," UNESCO, November 27, 2016, http://uis.unesco.org/en/country/gw; Bruneau, "The Guinea-Bissau Case."

41. African Development Bank, "Cape Verde: A Success Story," November 2012, https://www.afdb.org/sites/default/files/documents/projects-and-operations/cape_verde_-_a_success_story.pdf.

42. Peter Meyns, "Cape Verde: An African Exception," *Journal of Democracy* 13, no. 3 (2002): 153–65; Bruce Baker, "Cape Verde: The Most Democratic Nation in Africa?," *Journal of Modern African Studies*, 2006, 493–511.

43. Boal, "Mulheres de Abril."

44. António Tomás, *Amílcar Cabral: The Life of a Reluctant Nationalist* (London: Hurst & Co., 2021), 137; Lipinska, "Two Weeks With the Guinea-Bissau Liberation Army," 2.

45. Lipinska, "Two Weeks With the Guinea-Bissau Liberation Army," 17.

46. Amílcar Cabral and Richard Handyside, "Message to the People of Portugal" (Khartoum, 1969), available at https://www.marxists.org/subject/africa/cabral/1969/mpp.htm.

47. Lipinska, "Two Weeks With the Guinea-Bissau Liberation Army," 42.

48. Mendy, *Amílcar Cabral*, 64–65.

49. Reiland Rabaka, "Cabral's Critical Theory of Colonialism, Neocolonialism, and Imperialism," chapter 3 in *Concepts of Cabralism: Amilcar Cabral and Africana Critical Theory* (Lexington Books, 2014), 151–82.

50. José Javier Olivas Osuna, "The Deep Roots of the Carnation Revolution: 150 Years of Military Interventionism in Portugal," *Portuguese Journal of Social Science* 13, no. 2 (2014): 224.

51. António Tomás, "Introduction: Decolonising the 'Undecolonisable'? Portugal and the Independence of Lusophone Africa," *Social Dynamics* 42, no. 1 (January 2, 2016): 3, https://doi.org/10.1080/02533952.2016.1164956.

52. Osuna, "Deep Roots of the Carnation Revolution," 225.

53. Raquel Varela, "Today, We Celebrate the Carnation Revolution," interview by David Broder, *Jacobin*, April 25, 2019, https://jacobinmag.com/2019/04/portugal-carnation-revolution-national-liberation-april.

54. Tomás, "Decolonising the 'Undecolonisable'?"

55. Noam Chomsky, *Media Control: The Spectacular Achievements of Propaganda*, 2nd ed. (New York: Seven Stories Press, 2002), 20.

56. "Economic Justice," The Movement for Black Lives, https://policy.m4bl.org/.

57. Fantu Cheru, "Democracy and People Power in Africa: Still Searching for the 'Political Kingdom,'" *Third World Quarterly* 33, no. 2 (2012): 265–91; Jeffrey Williams, "The Pedagogy of Debt," *College Literature* 33, no. 4 (2006): 155–69.

58. Donella H. Meadows, *Thinking in Systems: A Primer* (Hartford, VT: Chelsea Green Publishing, 2008), 80.

59. Merrit Kennedy, "Lead-Laced Water In Flint: A Step-by-Step Look at the Makings of a Crisis," NPR, April 20, 2016, https://www.npr.org/sections/thetwo-way/2016/04/20/465545378/lead-laced-water-in-flint-a-step-by-step-look-at-the-makings-of-a-crisis.

60. Olúfẹ́mi O. Táíwò and Liam Kofi Bright, "A Response to Michael Walzer," *Dissent Magazine* (blog), https://www.dissentmagazine.org/online_articles/a-response-to-michael-walzer; Robin D. G. Kelley, "What Did Cedric Robinson Mean by Racial Capitalism?," *Boston Review*, January 12, 2017, https://bostonreview.net/race/robin-d-g-kelley-what-did-cedric-robinson-mean-racial-capitalism; Yousuf Al-Bulushi, "Thinking Racial Capitalism and Black Radicalism from Africa: An Intellectual Geography of Cedric Robinson's World-System," *Geoforum*, January 31, 2020, https://doi.org/10.1016/j.geoforum.2020.01.018.

61. Ole F. Norheim et al., "Difficult Trade-Offs in Response to COVID-19: The Case for Open and Inclusive Decision Making," *Nature Medicine* 27, no. 1 (January 1, 2021): 10–13, https://doi.org/10.1038/s41591-020-01204-6; Kyle Powys Whyte and Robert P. Crease, "Trust, Expertise, and the Philosophy of Science," *Synthese* 177, no. 3 (2010): 411–25; Gabriele Contessa, "It Takes a Village to Trust Science: Towards a (Thoroughly) Social Approach to Social Trust in Science" (unpublished research paper), 2021.

62. Micah Herskind, "Some Reflections on Prison Abolition after #MUMI," Medium, September 23, 2020, https://micahherskind.medium.com/some-reflections-on-prison-abolition-after-mumi-5197a4c3cf98.

63. Firoze Manji, "Amilcar Cabral and Ken Saro-Wiwa: Their Commonalities on Culture and the Struggle for Freedom," *Ukombozi Review* (blog), September 6, 2020, https://ukombozireview.com/blog/amilcar-cabral-and-ken-saro

-wiwa-their-commonalities-on-culture-and-the-struggle -for-freedom/.

64. Caroline Shenaz Hossein, *The Black Social Economy in the Americas: Exploring Diverse Community-Based Markets* (Springer, 2017); Caroline Shenaz Hossein, "Daring to Conceptualize the Black Social Economy," in *The Black Social Economy in the Americas* (Springer, 2018), 1–13; Jessica Gordon Nembhard, *Collective Courage: A History of African American Cooperative Economic Thought and Practice* (University Park: Penn State Press, 2014).

65. Joe William Trotter Jr., *Workers on Arrival: Black Labor in the Making of America* (Berkeley: University of California Press, 2019); Olúfẹ́mi O. Táíwò and Dylan Plummer, "Just Transition: Learning From the Tactics of Past Labor Movements," *The Trouble*, October 12, 2020, https://www.the-trouble.com /content/2020/10/12/just-transition-learning-from-the -tactics-of-past-labor-movements.

66. Urdang, "Fighting Two Colonialisms."

67. Anthony Faiola, "Egypt's Labor Movement Blooms in Arab Spring," *Washington Post*, September 25, 2011, https://www .washingtonpost.com/world/middle-east/egypts-labor -movement-blooms-in-arab-spring/2011/09/25/gIQAj6AfwK _story.html; "The Arab Spring and Independent Trade Unions: High Hopes and New Challenges—ITUC Survey of Violations of Trade Union Rights," Survey of Violations of Trade Union Rights, https://survey.ituc-csi.org/The -Arab-Spring-and-independent.html?lang=en; Urdang, "Fighting Two Colonialisms."

68. Dominika V. Polanska, Hannes Rolf, and Scott Springfeldt, "Tenants Organizing: Precarization and Resistance," Radical Housing Journal 3, no. 1 (2021): 121–29.

69. Jim Shultz, "The Cochabamba Water Revolt and Its Aftermath," in *Dignity and Defiance* (Berkeley: University of Cal-

ifornia Press, 2009), 9–44; Debt Collective, *Can't Pay, Won't Pay: The Case for Economic Disobedience and Debt Abolition* (Chicago: Haymarket Books, 2020).

70. Amilcar Cabral, "National Liberation and Culture" in *Return to the Source* (New York: Africa Information Service, 1973), 39–57.

71. Cabral, "National Liberation and Culture," 40–41, 43.

72. Cabral, "National Liberation and Culture," 51–52.

Chapter 5: The Point Is to Change It

1. Karl Marx, "Theses on Feuerbach," *Marx-Engels Selected Works*, vol. 1 (Moscow: Progress Publishers, 1969), 13–15.

2. Andaiye, "The Contemporary Caribbean Struggle," in *The Point Is to Change the World: Selected Writings of Andaiye*, Alissa Trotz, ed. (London: Pluto Press, 2020).

3. Clem Seecharan, "Foreword," in Andaiye, *The Point Is to Change the World.*

4. Andaiye, "Contemporary Caribbean Struggle."

5. Global Facility for Disaster Reduction and Recovery, "Stories of Impact: Communicating Flood Risk Along Guyana's Coast - Guyana." ReliefWeb, November 3, 2016, https://reliefweb.int /report/guyana/stories-impact-communicating-flood-risk -along-guyana-s-coast.

6. Ruth Wilson Gilmore, *Golden Gulag: Prisons, Surplus, Crisis, and Opposition in Globalizing California* (Berkeley: University of California Press, 2007), 176–78.

7. Keeanga-Yamahtta Taylor, *How We Get Free: Black Feminism and the Combahee River Collective* (Chicago: Haymarket Books, 2017), 117.

8. Briana Toole, "From Standpoint Epistemology to Epistemic Oppression," *Hypatia* 34, no. 4 (2019): 598–618; Briana Toole,

"Demarginalizing Standpoint Epistemology," *Episteme* 1 (2020): 19.

9. Agnes Callard, "The Philosophy of Anger," *Boston Review*, April 16, 2020, https://bostonreview.net/forum/agnes -callard-philosophy-anger.

10. Nick Estes (@nickwestes), Twitter, September 4, 2020, 4:40 pm, https://twitter.com/nickwestes/status /1301998637740851201.

11. Jane Howard, "Doom and Glory of Knowing Who You Are," *Life*, May 24, 1963.

Index

About the Author

© Jared Rodriguez

Olúfẹ́mi O. Táíwò is assistant professor of philosophy at Georgetown University. He received his PhD in philosophy at the University of California, Los Angeles. He has published in academic journals ranging from *Public Affairs Quarterly*, *One Earth*, *Philosophical Papers*, and the American Philosophical Association newsletter *Philosophy and the Black Experience*.

Táíwò's theoretical work draws liberally from the Black radical tradition, anti-colonial thought, German transcendental philosophy, contemporary philosophy of language, contemporary social science, and histories of activism and activist thinkers.

His public philosophy, including articles exploring intersections of climate justice and colonialism, has been featured in *The Nation*, *Boston Review*, *Dissent*, *The Appeal*, *Slate*, *Al Jazeera*, the *New Republic*, *Aeon*, and *Foreign Policy*.

He is the author of the book *Reconsidering Reparations*, published by Oxford University Press.

About Haymarket Books

Haymarket Books is a radical, independent, nonprofit book publisher based in Chicago.

Our mission is to publish books that contribute to struggles for social and economic justice. We strive to make our books a vibrant and organic part of social movements and the education and development of a critical, engaged, international left.

We take inspiration and courage from our namesakes, the Haymarket martyrs, who gave their lives fighting for a better world. Their 1886 struggle for the eight-hour day—which gave us May Day, the international workers' holiday—reminds workers around the world that ordinary people can organize and struggle for their own liberation. These struggles continue today across the globe—struggles against oppression, exploitation, poverty, and war.

Since our founding in 2001, Haymarket Books has published more than five hundred titles. Radically independent, we seek to drive a wedge into the risk-averse world of corporate book publishing. Our authors include Noam Chomsky, Arundhati Roy, Rebecca Solnit, Angela Y. Davis, Howard Zinn, Amy Goodman, Wallace Shawn, Mike Davis, Winona LaDuke, Ilan Pappé, Richard Wolff, Dave Zirin, Keeanga-Yamahtta Taylor, Nick Turse, Dahr Jamail, David Barsamian, Elizabeth Laird, Amira Hass, Mark Steel, Avi Lewis, Naomi Klein, and Neil Davidson. We are also the trade publishers of the acclaimed Historical Materialism Book Series and of Dispatch Books.

Also Available
from Haymarket Books

Abolition. Feminism. Now. by Angela Y. Davis, Gina Dent, Erica R. Meiners, and Beth E. Richie

Angela Davis: An Autobiography by Angela Y. Davis

Assata Taught Me: State Violence, Racial Capitalism, and the Movement for Black Lives by Donna Murch

Border and Rule: Global Migration, Capitalism, and the Rise of Racist Nationalism by Harsha Walia. afterword by Nick Estes, foreword by Robin D.G. Kelley

From #BlackLivesMatter to Black Liberation by Keeanga-Yamahtta Taylor, foreword by Angela Y. Davis

Speaking Out of Place: Getting Our Political Voices Back by David Palumbo-Liu

We Do This 'Til We Free Us: Abolitionist Organizing and Transforming Justice by Mariame Kaba, edited by Tamara K. Nopper, foreword by Naomi Murakawa

We Still Here: Pandemic, Policing, Protest, and Possibility by Marc Lamont Hill, edited by Frank Barat, foreword by Keeanga-Yamahtta Taylor